STEPPING INTO
GOD'S
PROMISES

For You

MUSA BAKO

Printed in the United States of America.

Library of Congress Control Number: 2023937391

ISBN   Paperback   979-8-88887-391-5
                eBook   979-8-88887-392-2

Westwood Books Publishing LLC
Atlanta Financial Center
3343 Peachtree Rd NE Ste 145-725
Atlanta, GA 30326

www.westwoodbookspublishing.com

CONTENTS

Introduction

The scriptures are filled with God's promises for believers. It is, therefore, necessary that every believer studies the scriptures to know these promises. Knowing the promises of God is of utmost importance because God gave believers His promises so that, through their fulfilment in a believer's life, he can escape the corruption in the world and partake of the divine nature.

> "Whereby are given unto us exceeding great and precious promises: that by these ye might be partakers of the divine nature, having escaped the corruption that is in the world through lust" (2 Peter 1:4 KJV).

Partaking in the divine nature means living the God kind of life. The God kind of life consists of having authority and exercising it over evil spirits, living in victory over the onslaught of Satan and his agents, spirit beings or humans, and living in the fullness of God's blessings. The corruption in the world speaks of things such as poverty and lack, sicknesses and diseases, failure and miseries, demons' control and manipulation, and all the vices of the enemy Satan. Suppose you know God's promises for you, and you step into them. In that case, your life will be revolutionised, you will know the freedom that Jesus speaks of in John 8:31-32, you will become a testimony of the reality of the power of the gospel to transform people and make them what God has always desired for people in Christ Jesus. Some of God's promises for believers, amongst others, include the following:

- The promise of being blessed and made a blessing - Hebrews 6: 13-18.
- The promise of provision - psalms 34:10; Romans 8:32; Philippians 4:19
- The promise of increase - Job 8: 7.
- The promise of a rich and fulfilled life - 2Timothy 1: 1; John 10:10.
- The promise of good health. Exodus 23:25.
- The blessing of healing- Jeremiah 30:17; 33:6; Exodus 15:26
- The promise of deliverance - proverbs 18:10; Psalms 121:7-8; 1Corinthians 10:13
- The promise of the fruit of the womb Exodus 23: 26.
- The promise of the gift of long life. Exodus 23: 26; psalms 91:16-16
- The promise of the Holy Spirit. Acts 1: 1; 2: 39.
- The promise of His presence - Isaiah 43:2; Psalms 23:4
- The promise of His leadership - Deuteronomy 31:8; proverbs 3:5-6
- The promise of protection. Isaiah 48: 17; Psalms 91: 3-8.
- The promise of His help - Isaiah 41:13
- The promise of eternal life. Hebrews 9: 15; 1John 2: 25.

There are loads of promises in the Scriptures for you to lay claim to, step into, and enjoy the goodness of God. All the promises in the Scriptures that God made across the two dispensations —the Old Testament and the New Testament—apply to the New Testament believers today. The new covenant is not short of any blessing that is in the Old Testament. The New Testament believers enjoy an even better and improved covenant compared to what was obtained in the old covenant.

> "But now hath he obtained a more excellent ministry, by how much also he is the mediator of a better covenant, which was established upon better promises. [7] For if that first covenant had been faultless, then should no place have been sought for the second." (Hebrews 8:6-7 KJV)

The new covenant was founded on a better promise because it includes the promises of redemption, eternal life, and the gift of the Holy Spirit, and it has a mediator and a surety, Jesus Christ, who obtained an excellent and eternal ministry and now sits at the right hand of God as guarantor of the fulfilment of the covenant promise in those who believe. All of these were not included in the old covenant.

> "But this man, because he continueth ever, hath an unchangeable priesthood. [25] Wherefore he is able also to save them to the uttermost that come unto God by him, seeing he ever liveth to make intercession for them" (Hebrews 7:24-25 KJV).

> Furthermore, we can see in Hebrews 6:13-17, that God had Abraham's heirs in mind when He made the promise of blessing to him, since in Christ Jesus you have become Abraham's heir, you can lay claim to every blessing God made to Abraham and his descendants (Romans 8:14-17; Galatians 3:29).

> "For when God made promise to Abraham because he could swear by no greater, he sware by himself, [14] Saying, Surely blessing I will bless thee, and multiplying I will multiply thee. [15] And so, after he had patiently endured, he obtained the promise. [16] For men verily swear by the greater: and an oath for confirmation is to them an end of all strife. [17] Wherein God, willing more abundantly to shew unto the heirs of promise the immutability of his counsel, confirmed it by an oath" (Hebrews 6:13-17 KJV).

God backed up the promise He made by sealing the promise with an oath. An oath is a human way of confirming the irrevocability of someone's promise, the genuineness of his heart, and the integrity of the word he spoke. Usually, an oath would bring to end all augments or contentions, as the bible has said, "People swear by someone greater than themselves, and the oath confirms what is said and puts an end to all argument" (Hebrews 6:16 NIV). The taking of oaths is immensely powerful. They invoke consequences in the case of deceit or failure to perform. In some cases, the consequences of non-performance could mean the death of the person. Making an oath implies that the person making the oath is, as it was in the oath's making, inviting someone greater than themselves, someone like a God who can bring judgment on the person who breaks the oath in the case of non-compliance. However, because God did not find anyone greater than Himself, He swore by Himself, making God himself the judge between Him and Abraham.

> "For when God made promise to Abraham, because he could swear by no greater, he sware by himself, [14] Saying, Surely blessing I will bless thee, and multiplying I will multiply thee." (Hebrews 6:13-14 KJV).

Abraham understood what God was doing when He swore an oath to him. He understood that God was using the language of men to convey the seriousness and unchangeable nature of His promise. Furthermore, by naming Himself as the judge between God and Abraham, God implied that He would condemn Himself if He failed to keep the oath He swore. We understand that God went this far not only for Abraham's sake. He swore an oath to assure Abraham's heirs, which include believers in Christ Jesus, of the immutability of His promises.

> "Wherein God, willing more abundantly to shew unto the heirs of promise the immutability of his counsel, confirmed it by an oath" (Hebrews 6:17 KJV).

Immutability is the state of being unable to change. When something is incapable of mutation, it means that it is constant. It means that the state or condition it is in today will be the state or condition it is in tomorrow. The promises of God are sure, they do not mutate. You to rest on it. You can take it to the bank. God did not swear an oath in order to commit Himself to His promise. Not at all. God is a promise-keeper. He is unchangeable and unwavering. Our God is a faithful, dependable, and a just God. He never fails. He swore an oath for Abraham's heirs' sake: to help them rest in confidence, trust, stand strong, and be unmoved irrespective of the circumstances or situations they find themselves in.

As you read the remaining eight chapters, I will be showing you the many ways you can engage God to actualize His promise for you and enjoy His goodness. I want you to know that it is never late with God. It is not too late for you to taste God's goodness. You must understand that your age does not matter, the things you have been through, and where you are at this stage in life do not matter. God can do something new and powerful in your life. I urge you to read this book prayerfully, believe God, and all you hold dear to your heart and are looking to God for shall happen, in the mighty name of Jesus.

GIVING MEN AND WOMEN THE
RESOURCES AND TOOLS, THEY
NEED TO SUCCEED IN LIFE AND
FULFIL THE REASON FOR WHICH
THEY WERE CREATED.

Chapter 1

GOD'S PROMISES ARE YES AND AMEN

"For as many as are the promises of God, in Christ they are [all answered] "Yes." So, through Him we say our "Amen" to the glory of God." (2 Corinthians 1:20 AMP)

A promise is only as good as the integrity of the person making it, and his capacity to keep it. It will be difficult to rely on a person's word if he is not known to keep it or if he is known to waver and be untrustworthy. Furthermore, no matter how trustworthy someone is, if he lacks the capacity to make what he promises happen, no matter how good his intentions are, the reality is that what he has promised is only a dream. The weight of any promise is measured by the integrity of the person keeping his word and the capacity of the person who makes the promise to fulfil it.

We can trust our God because we know that He is faithful and trustworthy. Also, according to the scriptures, He watches His word to perform it. Consider the following Scriptures:

"God is not a man, that he should lie; neither the son of man, that he should repent: hath he said, and shall he not do it? Or hath he spoken, and shall he not make it good?" (Number 23: 19 KJV)

1

"The LORD said to me, You have seen correctly, for I am watching to see that my word is fulfilled." (Jeremiah 1: 12 NIV)

For as many as are the promises of God, in Christ they are [all answered] "Yes." So, through Him we say our "Amen" to the glory of God." (2 Corinthians 1:20 AMP)

"Do not err, my beloved brethren. 17Every good gift and every perfect gift is from above, and cometh down from the Father of lights, with whom is no variableness, neither shadow of turning" (James 1: 16-17 KJV).

Furthermore, we can hold onto God's promises because we know that He is not only trustworthy, but He also has all power and the ability to make happen whatever He has said. He is the creator and can create anything. Consider the following scriptures:

"But Jesus beheld them, and said unto them, with men this is impossible; but with God all things are possible." (Matthew 19: 26 KJV).

"Then came the word of the LORD unto Jeremiah, saying, 27Behold, I am the LORD, the God of all flesh: is there anything too hard for me?" (Jeremiah 32: 26, 27 KJV)

"Ah Lord GOD! Behold, thou hast made the heaven and the earth by thy great power and stretched out arm, and there is nothing too hard for thee" (Jeremiah 32: 17 KJV)

Understand that it is never too late with God. If you are holding on to His word, He will bring it to pass because God does not fail. Someone might wonder, "If God never fails, how come the prophecy I received failed?" You are not alone in this. There are many people who are wondering and questioning, 'Why did God's promises failed? How come I am not walking in His blessing?' This is not a new thing, people have always asked the same question, dating back to man's experience of God. The story of Gideon is an excellent example. He also had questions concerning the promises God made to his ancestors. Gideon questioned the angel of God, asking why God would allow another nation to rule over Israel and His people, who appeared to him to commission him to fight to deliver Israel from their subjugation. The Bible in the book of Judges said, "And Gideon said unto him, Oh my Lord, if the Lord be with us, why then is all this befallen us? and where be all his miracles which our fathers told us of, saying, did not the Lord bring us up from Egypt? but now the Lord hath forsaken us, and delivered us into the hands of the Midianites." (Judges 6:13 KJV).

The experience of Gideon happened at a time when Israel was being subjugated by the Midianites. It so happened at the time that the Midianite people would invade Israel while they were harvesting their farms and would cater away with the produce, and Israel was powerless to defend itself. Gideon's experience could not be reconciled with God's promise of blessing and God's promise to make Israel the head and above all other nations. Furthermore, there are also people today, as there were in the early days of the church, who continue to question the promises of the second coming of Jesus. They think God failed because it has been over two thousand years since Jesus ascended to heaven and left us with a promise of His return, yet he has still not returned. Peter the apostle wrote about it, saying, "Knowing this first, that there shall come in the last days scoffers, walking after their own lusts, [4] And saying, where is the promise of his coming? for since the fathers fell asleep, all things continue as they were from the beginning of the creation" (2 Peter 3:3-4 KJV).

WHEN GOD'S PROMISES SEEMED TO HAVE FAILED

You must understand that God never fails. He is Holy and faithful to fail. Many things could be responsible wherever you observe or perceive that a promise of God has not been fulfilled. However, it would never be due to God's failure but rather to human factors. The following are a few reasons why God's promise may not materialize.

3

(1). What is being held as God's promise is based on false premise

This means that the promise of God that someone held or is holding is not grounded in the very word of GOD. In other words, God did not actually make such a promise. A good example here is my own experience when I had an accident several years ago. I questioned God over His promise of protection after the accident. I was asking to the Lord, why would you allow Satan to cause the accident? As if God did allow Satan. I said, "You should have protected me and not let this happen." I felt like God's promise of protection over me had failed. But then the Holy Spirit spoke to me so clearly, I could not have missed it. He said to me, "Son, I never said you will not pass through the waters, pass through the rivers, or walk through the fire, I said I will be with you through them all, and they will not overflow you, or burn you." (Isaiah 43:2-3). The Holy Spirit also said to me, "I never said no weapon will be formed against you, what I said is that no weapon formed against you shall prosper" (Isaiah 54:17). As the Holy Spirit spoke, those scripture verses came to me like a flashlight and took on so much meaning. God did keep His promise of protection to me that day. I did not understand that, that God is protecting me does not mean that the enemy Satan will not fight me. I came out of that accident without a scratch, surely God was with me every step of the way and He protected me from the harm Satan intended to cause.

Another area where people often question God's promises is when the word they are holding onto as a promise from God came by way of prophecy. Prophecy materialises only when someone says what God has said.

> "Who is he that saith, and it cometh to pass, when the Lord commandeth it not?" (Lamentations 3:37 KJV)

The new international version makes it even clearer. It says, "Who can speak and have it happened if the Lord has not decreed it?" (Lamentations 3:37). We are admonished in the scripture to not despise prophesying (1 Thessalonians 5:20). However, it also admonishes that we should prove

4

all things and only hold fast to that which is good (1 Thessalonians 5:21). As important as prophecy is in believers' lives, it is important to first understand that God does not intend for believers to base their entire future and life dealings on a prophecy. Everyone must develop intimacy with the Holy Spirit and learn to hear God concerning his own affairs by himself. Second, before you accept anything, you must first prove it. You are to judge the word spoken and be able to conclude that it is indeed a Word for you from God. You will make mistakes if you base the direction of your life entirely on a prophecy without first receiving confirmation of such a prophecy. Furthermore, if you claim to be holding on to a Scripture, you must ensure that you understand the Scripture in its context and that you have received a Rhema word from the said Scripture.

There is a difference between the written word and the Rhema word. Rhema is the spirit and life in the word, leaping out and speaking directly to you about a specific aspect of your life Rhema Word is the revelation knowledge breathed over you by the power of the Holy Spirit. The Holy Spirit breathes the word into you so that it comes alive, speaks directly to you and your situation, the scales fall off your face, you receive a new light, understand it differently than before, sense a new leading, and everything makes sense.

> "He has made us competent as ministers of a new covenant,
> not of the letter but of the Spirit; for the letter kills, but the
> Spirit gives life." (2 Corinthians 3:6 NIV)

A substantial proportion of the bible is a collection of stories of people's encounter with God and their exploits in their relationship with God. Those stories are written by the inspiration of God (2 Timothy 3:16), and they are also given to us for our admonition (1 Corinthians 10:11). The Holy Spirit will always give life to every scripture he uses in the present to speak to you, to provide you with a new leading. Other than that, you may only be operating in the realm of the letter. For instance, you cannot just say God told Joshua to go around Jericho's wall seven times and when he did, it came down crashing, so that must also be the promise of God for you as well, and you are also going to do what Joshua did, go round

5

your own city seven times and the city gates must be flung open for you. No, it will not work for you that way, except there is a specific leading by the Holy Spirit for you to do likewise. In the same vein, do not go around circling that property you are seeking to buy seven times and expect that the owner must sell it to you whether he likes it or not. And do not go circling around that company where you submitted your application for a job employment, expecting that they must employ you there, whether they like it or not because the wall of Jericho collapsed for Joshua, so the 'forces, contrary to you, in the company must yield to you as well. You are forgetting that what Joshua head was a Rhema word and may not be applicable to you today except GOD is saying for you to do same.

Always remember that the Holy Spirit needs to take the word, breathe life into it, and show it to you as revelation knowledge, for it to be your Rhema–God's Word to you. Any word you receive as Rhema and act upon will take form and become reality for you. There is a distinction between covenant Scriptures such as "by his stripes Ye are healed" and scriptures like "and the Lord said to David go for I shall deliver them into your hand." Understand that God was speaking to David and that is not for you to claim that scripture as your own. It must come to you as a Rhema Word first. Rhema Word is God speaking to you from His Word. God said those words to someone else before, but now he is saying them to you. He said to David, "go," but you can also hear the Word jumping out of the scriptures for you. It stands out for you, and it speaks directly to your situation. That's the Rhema Word for you!

(2). God's promise is not mixed with faith in those who receive it.

> "Let us therefore fear, lest, a promise being left us of entering into his rest, any of you should seem to come short of it. [2] For unto us was the gospel preached, as well as unto them: but the word preached did not profit them, not being mixed with faith in them that heard it." (Hebrews 4:1-2 KJV)

The scripture above talks about the over two million Jews who came out of Egypt with Moses to go to the land that God promised their fathers

Abraham, Isaac, and Jacob, the land of Canaan. Out of the two million people that God brought out of Egypt with a mighty hand, only Joshua and Caleb, from among those of warring age, entered the promised land. The rest perished in the wilderness. They all died in the wilderness and did not enter the land that God promised because they did not mix the promise with faith. To mix the promise of God with faith means to accept it as concrete and to act on it, obeying God's word concerning what He said about it. A word of prophecy or any message from the Lord spoken to someone can fall short, except when it is mixed with faith. To fall short of it is to fail to realize it. The promise of God, combined with the faith walk of the person who receives it, is what brings the promise of God to physical reality. Faith is the believer's lifeline. It is only by walking in faith that he can connect with God and have access to all the promises of God for him. God made a promise to Abraham and confirmed it with an oath. However, Abraham had to exercise his faith to see the reality of it.

> "That ye be not slothful, but followers of them who through faith and patience inherit the promises. [13] For when God made promise to Abraham because he could swear by no greater, he sware by himself, [14] Saying, surely blessing I will bless thee, and multiplying I will multiply thee. [15] And so, after he had patiently endured, he obtained the promise." (Hebrews 6:12-15 KJV)

Faith is the physical evidence that you have accepted what God said and are resting on it. Faith is more than what you accept in your heart, what you believe, or how you think. It is also about how you act, what you demonstrate, or what you do physically. Your faith is the real proof or evidence that, though you do not see something physically, you believe it is real and will become a physical reality. One fundamental aspect of faith is living in obedience to what God says.

> "And being made perfect, he became the author of eternal salvation unto all them that obey him; [10] Called of God an high priest after the order of Melchisedec." (Hebrews 5:8-10 KJV)

Obedience to God is what makes faith fundamentally different from belief. Anyone can believe in anything, but that does not make it faith. The Bible says even demons believe in God and tremble:

> "You believe that there is one God. You do well. Even the demons believe-and tremble! [20] But do you want to know, O foolish man, that faith without works is dead? [21] Was not Abraham our father justified by works when he offered Isaac his son on the altar?" (James 2:19-21 NKJV)

Yes, demons believe there is a God, but they do not live in obedience to God, they are rebels and workers of evil. There is no distinction between someone who only believes and is not living in harmony with God and demons who also believe. Believing is good, the confession of the word God is good, claiming God's promises is good. However, it is the doing of the Word that is faith. There is no faith without corresponding works or acting in obedience to what God says. A believer truly lives by faith when he or she walks in obedience to God. We can conclude that combining God's promises with faith means pursuing the promises while remaining in total obedience to God at all times. It is in walking in obedience to God that a believer experiences the reality of the work of salvation-God making good on His word in the believer's life.

(3). The promise of God that seemed failed was conditional upon someone doing something to make it happen

Many people want God to bless them, but they do not care about what God is telling them to do. A lot of what God will do in your life is conditional upon your doing something to make it happen. You have got to listen to what God is saying, do not ignore it. Never say God understands and He is a merciful God as an excuse for a disobedient lifestyle. Your obedience is critical to seeing the physical manifestation of what God said. You will be forfeiting a great deal by ignoring whatever God instructs you to do to make His word a physical reality in your life.

"If ye be willing and obedient, ye shall eat the good of the land" (Isaiah 1:19 KJV)

You must trust God and follow whatever He says. Do not ignore it. It is a tragedy for a believer to live life and not know what the Lord wants him to do or what the Lord is telling him to do. Knowing what God is saying and ignoring it is also self-destructive. Disobedience is a self-districting button. Do not just claim the promises of God. You must also understand what He is telling you to do in order for it to happen. Moreover, God is always seeking to teach you what to do to activate His blessing in your life.

"Thus, saith the Lord, thy Redeemer, the Holy One of Israel; I am the Lord thy God which teacheth thee to profit, which leadeth thee by the way that thou shouldest go. [18] O that thou hadst hearkened to my commandments! then had thy peace been as a river, and thy righteousness as the waves of the sea: [19] Thy seed also had been as the sand, and the offspring of thy bowels like the gravel thereof; his name should not have been cut off nor destroyed from before me." (Isaiah 48:17-19 KJV).

When you claim a promise from God, you must seek to understand what God is telling you to do to make it a reality. Do not just confess Scripture and pray in the Spirit. As much as these are very potent, they cannot cover your ignorance of what to do, your insensitivity to the Holy Spirit, or disobedience to the Lord.

(4). Contamination could have interrupted or hindered the performance of the promise

The sinful contamination of a believer's body can give Satan access to him. If Satan can gain access to any place, he will ruin things there. He is a spoiler of anything good, and he is always on the lookout for an opportunity to do so. Jesus said:

"The thief cometh not, but for to steal, and to kill, and to destroy: I am come that they might have life, and that they might have it more abundantly." (John 10:10 KJV)

Because of God's promises to us, we are admonished in the scripture to keep ourselves pure and free of contamination.

"Therefore, since we have these promises, dear friends, let us purify ourselves from everything that contaminates body and spirit, perfecting holiness out of reverence for God." (2 Corinthians 7:1 NIV).

The admonition in 2 Corinthians 7:1 would not be necessary if contamination has no effect on the promise of God. Satan likes to mess things up for believers. He knows that he can only achieve it if he can get believers contaminated by sin. Satan is no fool, he is fully aware that nothing happens until the Holy Spirit moves and quickens their manifestation. The Bible says, "It is the spirit that quickeneth; the flesh profiteth nothing: the words that I speak unto you, they are spirit, and they are life." (John 6:63 KJV). Satan was aware that even Jesus, though the son of God, could do nothing by himself and He performed wonderful things in His life and ministry through the help of the Holy Spirit, for the Bible says,

"How God anointed Jesus of Nazareth with the Holy Spirit and power, and how he went around doing good and healing all who were under the power of the devil, because God was with him." (Acts 10:38 NIV)

Furthermore, it was also through the quickening of the Holy Spirit that Jesus was raised from the death (1 Peter 3:18). The Holy Spirit is the power through which God will make anything come into being. He is the force behind all creation. If the Holy Spirit is not moving, nothing happens. The quickest way for anyone to obstruct the Holy Spirit's work in their lives is to grieve him, that is, to obstruct his work by submitting to a sinful lifestyle. Therefore, the Bible is saying to not grieve the Holy

Spirit (Ephesians 4:27-31). It is the Holy Spirit that births and brings forth all of God's promises. According to the scripture, the in dwelling of the Holy Spirit in believers is the guarantee that they will come into God's inheritance, which He promised.

> "The Spirit is God's guarantee that he will give us the inheritance he promised and that he has purchased us to be his own people. He did this so we would praise and glorify him" (Ephesians 1:14 NLT)

Ignoring the Holy Spirit and putting Him to grief through disobedient living is detrimental to the believer. So be aware that living a sinful lifestyle will cost the believer a great deal. He will be forfeiting his covenant blessing. Satan will be able to make him a cheap pray, will get in the way, and will be successful in preventing many good things from happening. Healing, in particular is one of God's promises that sin contamination stands in the way of. You may fast and pray, but you may never be healed if you do not repent and change your lifestyle. Jesus referred to sin a few times and its effect on healing when he engaged in healing people:

> "Afterward Jesus findeth him in the temple, and said unto him, Behold, thou art made whole: sin no more, lest a worse thing come unto thee." (John 5:14 KJV)

Remember that sin contamination is an enemy of healing and Divine health because it allows Satan to enter your life. Never toy with sin, and never make excuses for it. Quickly get up whenever there is a fall, and do not let Satan have any advantage over you.

(5). The promise did not really fail, it only tarried

The promise of God tarrying means that it did not take a physical form and manifest at the time it was meant to happen. It is possible for the promise of God to linger and not happen when it was meant to happen. For instance, God told Abraham that his descendants would be slaves in Egypt for four hundred years (Genesis 15:13; Acts 7:6), but it took them four hundred and thirty years to be free (Exodus 12:40-41). In the light of God's promise to Abraham, his descendants overstayed their time in Egypt by thirty years. The following are some of the reasons why God's promises may tarry:

(I).   God's promises can sometimes be delayed because God is waiting for the person to whom the promise is made to meet the condition that will trigger the blessing. When the promise is contingent on someone doing something first, the fulfilment will linger until there is performance on the person's part. A lot of the times that Israel's deliverance and the prosperity of their nation were delayed, it was because they failed to do what God commanded them to do. God had said to Moses that Israel's blessing would be conditional upon its compliance with God's command.

> "if only you fully obey the Lord your God and are careful to follow all these commands I am giving you today. [6] For the Lord your God will bless you as he has promised, and you will lend to many nations but will borrow from none. You will rule over many nations but none will rule over you." (Deuteronomy 15:5-6 NIV).

Think about this, what would have happened to Naaman's leprosy (2 Kings 5:10-14), the widow of Zarephath's supply (1 Kings 17:8-1), and the blind man's healing (John 9:1-7), if they all ignored to do what they were instructed to do to get their breakthrough? Willingness to be healed or blessed is not enough, obedience is very critical (Isaiah 1:19).

(II). Sometimes God's promises tarry because the person it was given to failed to grow to the stage where he can receive it.

> "Now I say, That the heir, as long as he is a child, differeth nothing from a servant, though he be lord of all; [2] But is under tutors and governors until the time appointed of the father." (Galatians 4:1-2 KJV).

The believer in Christ Jesus is an heir of God, entitling to enjoy the Father God's blessings (Galatians 4:6-7). You are meant to walk in the fullness of that which God promises and enjoy His goodness. However, as heir you are required to develop yourself, grow and mature (Jude 1:20), for you to be able to get access to your inheritance in Christ Jesus.

> "Now I say, That the heir, as long as he is a child, differeth nothing from a servant, though he be lord of all" (Galatians 4:1 KJV)

Understand that walking into your inheritance is dependent on you growing up. You must build yourself up, as the Scripture instructs.

> "But you, beloved, building yourselves up on your most holy faith, praying in the Holy Spirit" (Jude 1:20 NKJV)

God is interested in your whole body, spirit, and soul. You are to develop and grow in every aspect of your life, and no one aspect should be left stunted.

> "And the very God of peace sanctify you wholly; and I pray God your whole spirit and soul and body be preserved blameless unto the coming of our Lord Jesus Christ." (1 Thessalonians 5:23 KJV)

There are many things God will not bring into your life if you haven't grown yet because you will not be able to handle them by reason of your lack of growth. The apostle Paul said also that the lack of growth is a reason some people are being tossed to and from, and are easily being deceived by fake and lying prophets.

> "That we henceforth be no more children, tossed to and fro, and carried about with every wind of doctrine, by the sleight of men, and cunning craftiness, whereby they lie in wait to deceive" (Ephesians 4:14 KJV)

These so-called prophets prophesy lies, make unfounded promises, and make merchandise of you. You believe them, and you give them huge amounts of your hard-earned money as seeds, but unfortunately, what you held on to is based on a false premise and is never going to happen.

You must pay attention on building yourself up; the Bible says, "But you, beloved, building yourselves up on your most holy faith…" (Jude 1:20 NKJV). Spiritual development is the most important investment anyone can make. Your spirituality is the foundation upon which everything else will be determined, including the quality of your relationship with God and the manifestation of the things He has in store for you. If you do not develop and mature spiritually, you will be:

(a). Spiritually weak and powerless
(b). Spiritually ignorant
(c). spiritually blind

If you are spiritually weak and blinded, you will be completely ignorant of the satanic devises around you and will become his constant victim, being played about as a football. Some of the indicators that someone is not spiritually developed and is weak include:

(i).   prayerlessness
(ii).   not having the passion for spiritual things
(iii). not being able to hear and discern the voice of the Holy Spirit
(iv).   having struggles with church attendance
(v).   keeping of malice and holding back forgiveness
(vi).   loss of hunger for the word of God
(vii). making excuses for sins.

The one fundamental way to build yourself up spiritually is to devote yourself to the study of the word of God. Paul the apostle wrote admonishing the church saying, "And now, brethren, I commend you to God, and to the word of his grace, which is able to build you up, and to give you an inheritance among all them which are sanctified" (Acts 20:32 KJV). Have an insatiable craving for the Word. Treat the word of God as though your life is dependent on it. It is not possible to grow not being committed to studying the Word (1 Peter 2:2). If you are committed to your spiritual development, you must also be committed to feeding on the Word. You cannot have it another way.

(III). Sometimes the promises of God tarry because the enemy, Satan, is resisting their physical manifestation. The believer must not be ignorant of the devices of Satan. The believer needs to pray God's promises through and take nothing for granted. Just because God said so does not mean that Satan will not try to stop it. The Israelites overstayed God's timing for them in Egypt by thirty years because they initially held back and relaxed, but when they groaned and cried to God for their deliverance, He sent them a deliverer by the name of Moses.

> "And the Lord said, I have surely seen the affliction of my people which are in Egypt, and have heard their cry by reason of their taskmasters; for I know their sorrows; [8] And I am come down to deliver them out of the hand of the Egyptians, and to bring them up out of that land unto a good land and a large, unto a land flowing with milk and honey; unto the place of the Canaanites, and the Hittites, and the Amorites, and the Perizzites, and the Hivites, and the Jebusites. [9] Now therefore, behold, the cry of the children of Israel is come unto me: and I have also seen the oppression wherewith the Egyptians oppress them. [10] Come now therefore, and I will send thee unto Pharaoh, that thou mayest bring forth my people the children of Israel out of Egypt (Exodus 3:7-10 KJV).

There are forces that are opposed to you and are constantly fighting to resist the materialization of God's blessings in your life. The Bible records that Daniel's prayer was answered the very first day he started praying. However, a principality in the form of the prince of Persia held back the angel that God sent to deliver the answer to Daniel for twenty-one days. Daniel would not have received the answer if he had not prayed through, and if his prayers had not sustained the angel.

"Then he continued, "Do not be afraid, Daniel. Since the first day that you set your mind to gain understanding and to humble yourself before your God, your words were heard, and I have come in response to them. [13] But the prince of the Persian kingdom resisted me twenty-one days. Then Michael, one of the chief princes, came to help me, because I was detained there with the king of Persia. [14] Now I have come to explain to you what will happen to your people in the future, for the vision concerns a time yet to come." (Daniel 10:12-14 NIV)

You must learn to pray through God's promises for you. Do not just sit tight, folding your hands and doing nothing about it. Devote yourself to fasting and prayer, engage in a warfare to release your blessing anytime you sense a delay, and or a demonic interference in what God is doing in your life. Even Jesus had to pray through in the garden of Gethsemane to defeat the satanic forces working against the death on the cross for redemption sacrifice, otherwise the work of redemption would not have been completed (Mathew 26:36-46)

(IV). Sometimes the promise of God may have tarried due to God's timing. In this instance, the promise of God is only appearing to be tarrying, but it is not tarrying. The promise did not materialise physically at the time you thought it should have, because it is not yet the time for it as far as God's timing is concerned. God has an appointed time for everything He does.

> "Is there not an appointed time to man upon earth? are not his days also like the days of an hireling?" (Job 7:1 KJV)

We must pray for God to reveal to us the season of our harvest so that we can pray through it. Even though it appeared that God's promise of a son for Abraham had been delayed, it was not because the promise was that God would visit Sarah at the appointed time. For the scripture says, "For this was how the promise was stated: "At the appointed time I will return, and Sarah will have a son." (Romans 9:9 NIV). The birth of Isaac was to happen at the appointed time, and God visited Sarah as He promised.

> "And the Lord visited Sarah as he had said, and the Lord did unto Sarah as he had spoken. [2] For Sarah conceived, and bare Abraham a son in his old age, at the set time of which God had spoken to him" (Genesis 21:1-2 KJV).

Also, concerning the second coming of Jesus, we can see from the scripture that it is not a failed promise. Jesus is only being long-suffering and holding back from His return for the sake of the elect. The Bible says,

> "The Lord is not slack concerning his promise, as some men count slackness; but is longsuffering to us-ward, not willing that any should perish, but that all should come to repentance. "(2 Peter 3:9).

There are many people out there in the world, elected by God, who are yet to know Him. They need to hear about God's offer of salvation before the return of Jesus. A lot of the elect of the Lord who are still not saved are not saved because they have not been spoken to about Jesus, personally, in the simplicity of the gospel, and in a manner in which they are able to understand the gospel message and make an informed decision. Some of these people are not believers because they were raised by atheists parents who taught them that God does not exist and that even if He does, He does not care about them.

God does not want these elect to perish, and therefore, Jesus is being long suffering, holding back His return for their sake. God is giving them more time so they can have the gospel preached to them and be saved and brought into His kingdom. There are many people who are not born again and are not saved because nobody has really told them about Jesus in a way that they could understand the gospel message. It is every believer's duty to reach out to these people. As you are reading this book, I pray that the Holy Spirit will move you to start doing something about the people around you who are not saved. Everyone you meet who is not saved is a potential heir of the kingdom of Jesus.

Understanding the timing of things is particularly important in your walk to your destiny. If you have no clue about time, if you do not understand the timing of things, you may ruin the process of birthing something, and hinder the manifestation. If you do not understand the timing of things, you will think that your time has passed, accept defeat, and accept your circumstance as finality. But how can your circumstance be a finality when God's promises are still hanging? The next chapter is about time, and there are more things about time you will discover as you go through it.

WHEN GOD DOES CHANGE HIS MIND AND ALLOW HIS PROMISE TO FAIL

In closing this chapter, I must let you know that God changes his mind about his promise and may allow it fail, but only when it is attached to a condition, and the condition is not met by the person who received the promise. An excellent example for us is the story of Eli, the priest of God. It is on record that God changed His mind about continuing the priesthood with His children because Eli neglected to do as the Lord commanded him, and his children became dishonouring to God and did things in disregard of Him.

> "Wherefore the LORD God of Israel saith, I said indeed that thy house, and the house of thy father, should walk before me forever: but now the LORD saith, Be it far from me; for them that honour me I will honour, and they that despise me shall be lightly esteemed. (1 Samuel 1: 30 KJV).

You must honor God in your life if you want Him to keep His word and bring you into a position of honor. The Golden rule, "Do to others whatever you would like them to do to you" (Matthew 7:12), also applies in our relationships with God. God cannot honour you and reveal His power in you if you show Him no honour and hold him in disregard. Another good case study is how God promised the land of Canaan to the two million people that came out of Egypt with Moses. He brought them out with a mighty hand to take them into the land He promised. However, only two people who were of warring age at the time they left Egypt entered the Promised Land. The others perished in the wilderness, not having received the promise. God put their experience of coming short of His promise in the scripture for our example:

> "Let us therefore fear, lest a promise being left us of entering into his rest, any of you should seem to come short of it. [2] For unto us was the gospel preached, as well as unto them: but the word preached did not profit them, not being mixed with faith in them that heard it." (Hebrews 4:1-2 KJV).

God promised the land of Canaan to the people that perished in the wilderness, as well as Joshua and Caleb. However, they did not enter the Promised Land. They did not receive the promise of a city with houses that they did not build as God promised. They did not receive the promise of vineyards, which they did not plant themselves as promised. They did not see the promise of a land that flows with milk and honey fulfilled in their lives. The Word that God gave them did not benefit them. The Bible says the Word spoken did not benefit them because they did not do what was required of them to do to make God's promises happen to them. They were required to mix the word with faith, but they failed to do so.

I have seen in my years of ministry, how the word of God spoken to many people in church, through a prophetic utterance, under an extraordinarily strong anointing, by word of wisdom or word of knowledge but sadly the words spoken did not profit some people that heard it. It did not change the people's lives. It had no impact because they did nothing with what they heard.

I have seen people come to church and take their seat each week for years, under a strong teaching anointing, but their lives are not improving;

They are not getting healed
Their finance situation is not improving
Their marriage is not getting better
Their enemies are attacking them and are succeeding
They are losing businesses
They are not making profits
Their investment is collapsing
They hear about uncommon favour, but it never happened to them
And it seems like in them the word of God is void of power.

However, the word of God is not void of power. The word and promises of God are yes and amen, they happen. But for them to happen, there are certain things you need to know and do to make room for God to bring them to pass in your life. This book you are holding will show you in the following chapters the steps you must take to step into God's promises for you. I encourage you to go through the chapters prayerfully and receive with simplicity whatever God is saying to you.

Chapter 2

THERE IS AN APPOINTED TIME

Your appointment time is your pay day from the Lord, the day He has set to visit your case. God does everything at the time of His choosing, and not ours. The Bible says, "Is there not an appointed time to man upon earth? are not his days also like the days of an hireling?" (Job 7:1 KJV). The way Heaven functions in the affairs of man are like the relationship between an employer and an employee, or the farm owner and the hireling. A hireling is paid on a particular day, usually called the pay day. Many things can happen in the interim, that is, between the start of work and pay day. For instance, as in a typical workplace, your work conditions may become a little harder, and you may have to deal with unreasonable colleagues. Likewise, it could get tough in the period between now and the day your miracle will come through for you, such that you may wonder why your prayers have not been answered yet or why the fasting, the tithing, and the seed of faith seem not to be yielding results for you. That in-between season can be extremely difficult. You can ask the Lord to help you understand the timing of your pay day and pray for grace to wait patiently for it.

In dealing with God, the pay day may not be the time you expect it to be. Therefore, praying for grace to wait patiently for the day is important. That was what Abraham did, and He waited for it and got his promise fulfilled. The Bible says of him, "and so, after he had patiently endured, he obtained the promise." (Hebrews 6:13-15 KJV). When it is not your pay day, you may be seeking your healing, and your doctors will be confused about what is wrong with your body. When it is not your pay day yet, your friends will be asking why you are still where you are and have not improved. When it is not your pay day yet, even your enemies will be laughing at you. Someone reading this book may be in that situation where nothing is going as planned. Possibly:

(a). You are finding life hard to live.

(b). You are financially broke and finding it difficult to pay the bills.

(c). You have finished school a long time ago, but no decent job has come through for you, and it seems like your education is becoming a waste.

(e). You are single and concerned about your marriage. It has tarried, and friends and family are constantly reminding you that you are not growing any younger.

(d). The business you started and have invested so much into seems to be failing, and you cannot afford to lose your investment.

(f). You feel alone and neglected by people you once helped, and you are saying to the Lord 'please remember me.'

No matter what the situation is, I would like to announce to you that your set time will come soon. The Lord has not forgotten you, and He will not. It is not in His character to forget. This is what the Lord said:

> "Never! Can a mother forget her nursing child? Can she feel
> no love for the child she has borne? But even if that were
> possible, I would not forget you!" (Isaiah 49:15 NLT)

Your enemies may be laughing at you. Your family, your neighbours, and your friends may be looking at you as a failure, however, I declare over you in the mighty name of Jesus that the set time for your breakthrough is here, right now. Do not let the devil lie to you and tell you that God has forgotten you, or that He has something against you, that you are under a curse. I announce to you that God has not forgotten you, He is concerned about your situation, He has not rejected you, neither is He against you. If you are born again, I assure you, by God, that there is no curse on you. Your situation is neither the problem of a curse nor a rejection from God. Not at all. It is all about the appointed time, which will come. It is said that delay is not denial.

> "Is there not an appointed time to man upon earth? are not his days also like the days of an hireling?" (Job 7:1 KJV)

The pay day is also called the day of God's visitation. Yes, God visits people, and He will visit you too. The psalmist wrote:

> "What is man, that thou art mindful of him? and the son of man, that thou visitest him" (Psalm 8:4 KJV).

The very day that God visited Sarah was the day she was conceived, and the age she had reached did not matter.

And the Lord visited Sarah as he had said, and the Lord did unto Sarah as he had spoken. [2] For Sarah conceived, and bare Abraham a son in his old age, at the set time of which God had spoken to him." (Genesis 21:1-2 KJV).

GOD HAS SET A TIME FOR YOU.

It appeared like God had forgotten to bless Abraham with a son through Sarah as He promised, for Sarah had advanced in age and had become an old woman. God has a set time for everything He does, and He is never too early or late. Everyone who knew Abraham and Sarah and their faith in Jehovah must have wondered where they got it wrong. However, God had a set time when He was going to visit Sarah, and He will fulfil His word to Abraham. Of course, God visited her at the set time, and it did not matter that Sarah was long past the age of having children. She got pregnant according to what God promised. The Bible records:

> "And the Lord visited Sarah as he had said, and the Lord did unto Sarah as he had spoken. [2] For Sarah conceived, and

23

bare Abraham a son in his old age, at the set time of which God had spoken to him." (Genesis 21:1-2 KJV).

The day God visits someone, His glory will begin to manifest upon the person, and his breakthrough will happen in a way he never expects. What appeared impossible will become a reality, and without much effort. The long-awaited healing will come through, no matter what doctors have said about it. The person who was rejected in a place before, when he is visited by God, God's glory will shine upon him, he will experience a sudden turnaround of events, and he would be received and celebrated in the same place they rejected him, and yes, without him doing anything different to change people's perception. I assure you that God will always answer prayers that line up with his will, He will always fulfil His promises. However, never forget that He does everything at the time he has set. He will visit you when it is your time.

Abraham's story tells us that no matter how long it takes, no matter the age someone has advanced to, it will be immaterial in the light of God's visitation. When it is your pay day, your breakthrough will take place (Genesis 18:1,9-10; Genesis 21:1-2). Abraham and Sarah's story is a testimony that God can restore anything. He can restore dead marriages. He can restore lost relationships. He can empower the barren to conceive and bring forth her children. He can bring life where death has occurred. He can put a pauper on the throne. He has the ability to make a homeless to a company director. No matter how old someone is, God can empower him or her to have their baby. All it takes is a visitation from the Lord. God will visit you at His set time for you.

GOD'S DAY OF VISITATION IS LIFE TRANSFORMING

David's experience shows us that when it is someone's time to be blessed, even his family's opinion of him will not matter, and nothing can hinder God (1 Samuel 16:1-13). David's family left him out, he was not considered as fit for the throne. However, God fished him out even though he was left out because it was his visitation time. Here is the lesson to take from

David's story, When it is your set time, it will not really matter what anybody thinks of you. When it is your set time, it will not really matter what anybody is saying about you. People may think you don't qualify, they may think you do not deserve it, they may think you are too old or too young for it, they may think you are not holy enough, and do not fast and pray enough. However, when it is your time all that do not count before God who qualifies us.

Elisha's story is another example we can learn from. God's visitation to Elisha right in the farm shows us that the location you are at may not matter with God, He can meet you and raise you up irrespective of your location (1 Kings 19:15-19). Elisha was anointed to replace Elijah as the prophet of God in Israel. God met him and anointed him while he was working on his farm. Elisha was not in the temple fasting, praying, and worshipping. He was not in the spirit; he was on the farm working, but it did not matter because it was his visitation day.

Another beautiful example is the story of the impotent man at Bethesda pool (John 5:2-9). This man's tragedy was not the length of time he was in his problems. His tragedy was that he had no one–no friend, no family that was caring enough, supportive enough, and willing to help thrust him into the pool at the stirring of the water by an angel. He was only surrounded by people who only cared about themselves, but they also wanted what he was there for and competed with him in his quest for healing. He was impotent. He was Helpless. He was Weak. He needed a helping hand to get into the pool, but there was no human being willing to help. However, on the day of his set time for visitation, Jesus came looking for him. He did not go looking for Jesus, instead Jesus came looking for him, and he did not have to jump into any water. God had alternative plans for him. I see a divine help coming someone's way. You will not have to do anything to deserve it. I speak God's word over you right now, wherever you are, and I decree and declare your breakthrough in the mighty name of Jesus. Sometimes you really do not have to go all over the place scouting for men of God to pray for you and anoint you with oil. I see Jesus touching you right now, right there.

IMPORTANT STEPS FORWARD FOR YOU TO CONSIDER

There are three things I'd like you to take note of as I draw this chapter to a close:

(1). Continue to walk in the consciousness of God's promises over you, and never let the devil lie to you that God has failed, that your time has passed, or that yours has always been only a pipe dream. You need to keep reminding yourself through meditation and confession of the word, giving glory to God for His ability and faithfulness to bring to pass His good counsel concerning you.

> "And being not weak in faith, he considered not his own body now dead, when he was about an hundred years old, neither yet the deadness of Sarah's womb: 20He staggered not at the promise of God through unbelief; but was strong in faith, giving glory to God; 21And being fully persuaded that, what he had promised, he was able also to perform. 22And therefore it was imputed to him for righteousness". (Romans 4: 19-22 KJV)

(2). Consider sowing a seed of faith, from time to time, towards the manifestation of your expectation. God said, "Remind me concerning the works of my hand." Your offerings and prayers combined come before God as memorial, or for remembrance.

> "And when he looked on him, he was afraid, and said, what is it, Lord? And he said unto him, thy prayers and thine alms are come up for a memorial before God." (Acts 10:4 KJV)

(3). Keep standing your ground, keep holding on, and keep waiting for your time (2 Peter 1: 5; Galatians 3: 14; Romans 4: 16-21). No matter what happens to you in the interim, and no matter what you hear people say or what whispers come to your hearing, you have got to hold fast to what God has said about you, do not let go.

The devil will test your faith by doing things to you to test your belief in what you are claiming. He may try to complicate your situation by attacking you, making it look like God is doing nothing about it. He may incite others to say disparaging things about your stance on the word you received. Listen, your situation may even become worse, but it will get better if you do not get moved.

> "Cast not away therefore your confidence, which hath great recompence of reward. [36] For ye have need of patience, that, after ye have done the will of God, ye might receive the promise. [37] For yet a little while, and he that shall come will come, and will not tarry." (Hebrews 10:35-37).

Paying attention to verse 36 of the scripture above, you would see that you need to have patience and be in obedience to the will of God to receive His promise. Being patient is the key here. It indicates that you are holding your ground. I have dedicated a whole chapter to faith and patience, I am not going to dwell much on it here. While patience is indicative of perseverance, the proof that you are persevering is seen in your continued obedience to God's will. Keep on doing the will of God no matter how frustrated you feel.

Chapter 3

THE PRINCIPLE OF SEEDTIME AND HARVEST

"While the earth remaineth, seedtime and harvest, and cold and heat, and summer and winter, and day and night shall not cease." (Genesis 8:22 KJV)

Seed time and harvest are eternal principles. It will never cease if there is human existence here on earth. It is the law that governs life's replication, reproduction, increase, and expansion. Everything that is living will eventually die and become extinct without the Principles of Seedtime and harvest in play. This is how Jesus puts it:

"Verily, verily, I say unto you, except a corn of wheat fall into the ground and die, it abideth alone: but if it die, it bringeth forth much fruit." (John 12:24 KJV).

Where there is no seed planted, there will be no harvest time. And when there is no harvest, whatever is left will start to diminish and will eventually be used to extinction. You must make the sowing of seed your lifestyle and not something you do occasionally. It is the way of life that God ordained for people to sustain things, grow them, and make them increase. It is good to pray about your needs, but you must learn to combine your prayer with the planting of seeds because a lot of the things you desire will require you to also plant seed to reap their harvest. Prayer and planting seeds are powerful together. An angel came to a certain man by the name of Corneilus, and he says to him, thy prayers and thine alms are brought up for a memorial before God (Acts 10:1-4)? Do not just pray, back your prayers with the seed; it will birth something for you. It is important to know what seed you need to plant and for what harvest. No farmer goes to the farm bearing seeds without knowing what type of seed they are carrying or the kind of harvest they are planting for. You must plant your seed with a specific goal in mind.

NAMING YOUR SEED AND YOUR HARVEST

> "Be not deceived; God is not mocked: for whatsoever a man soweth, that shall he also reap"(Galatians 6:7 KJV).

There is a connection between your seed and your harvest. Usually, it is what you sow that you are going to harvest. For instance, if you sow corn, you reap corn and not rice. In the same vein, you do not harvest wheat where you planted corn. In like manner, if you want the harvest of kindness, you will need to sow kindness, and if you seek forgiveness, love, mercy, etc., you will also need to give them out to people as seeds. You have the right to reap the benefits of forgiveness if you give it. This is what Jesus said about it:

> "But if ye do not forgive, neither will your Father which is in heaven forgive your trespasses" (Mark 11:26 KJV).

The law of Seedtime and harvest applies to all aspects of human life. It works in spiritual things as well as in material things because it is both a natural law and a spiritual law. The principle of Seedtime and harvest impacts all aspects of human relationships and dealings. This is also what is referred to as the *golden rule,* coined in Matthew 7:12.

> "Therefore, all things whatsoever ye would that men should do to you, do ye even so to them: for this is the law and the prophets." (KJV)

29

The golden rule operates under the law of Seedtime and harvest. It is said that one good turn deserves another. What you do to others will always be returned to you. Whatever you give away will return to you as a harvest. If you are giving away shoes, ties, suits, cars, and money, you will have a harvest of them, people will start to give them to you. Harvests usually do not come in the quantity of the seed planted. They are usually in greater measure:

> "Give, and it will be given to you. A good measure, pressed down, shaken together and running over, will be poured into your lap. For with the measure you use, it will be measured to you." (Luke 6:38 NIV)

The Harvest of the seed you planted will come in greater quantities than what you planted. The phrase "For with the measure you use, it will be measured to you" simply means that if you sow liberally or bountifully, the harvest will also be bountifully, and if your seed is sown sparingly, the harvest will come sparingly. The harvest will always be more than the seed sown, but the degree and quantity of the harvest will be determined by your level of generosity in the planting. In other words, the person who planted a full bag of wheat is likely to have a larger harvest than the person who only planted half a bag of wheat.

> "But this I say, He which soweth sparingly shall reap also sparingly; and he which soweth bountifully shall reap also bountifully." (2 Corinthians 9:6 KJV)

In naming your seed and the harvest, I am also showing you that you can apply the law of Seedtime and harvest to sow into any harvest, even if the harvest is something different from the seed you sowed. I want you to be aware that the law of Seedtime and harvest is both a spiritual law as well as a natural law. By "natural law," I mean it takes a natural course, like the planting of wheat for the harvest of wheat. However, it does not follow the name pattern spiritually. In the spiritual dimension, you may not necessarily have a harvest of a car simply because you gave out a car. The harvest can come in other forms. For instance, you can sow your shoes, your handbag, your money, or anything and believe in the harvest of employment, fruit of the womb, healing, an open door to financial increase, etc. We see that in the experience of Cornelius in Acts 10:1-4; his arms giving to support the works in the Jewish synagogue, and him helping the poor among them, pave the way for him to have an angelic visit and the experience of salvation.

Another good example of what I am saying here is the story about the Shunammite woman's act of kindness in 2 Kings 4:8-17. This woman built a chamber for the prophet Elisha, and we see that in this case also, God did not give her the harvest of houses. Instead, He gave her the harvest of a baby son. The most important need in her life at the time was to have a child. God saw it, and He rewarded her gift of Elisha's chamber with a son.

> "And it fell on a day, that Elisha passed to Shunem, where was a great woman; and she constrained him to eat bread. And so it was, that as oft as he passed by, he turned in thither to eat bread. [9] And she said unto her husband, behold now, I perceive that this is an holy man of God, which passeth by us continually. [10] Let us make a little chamber, I pray thee, on the wall; and let us set for him there a bed, and a table, and a stool, and a candlestick: and it shall be, when he cometh to us, that he shall turn in thither. [11] And it fell on a day, that he came thither, and he turned into the chamber, and lay there. [12] And he said to Gehazi his servant, Call this Shunammite. And when he had called her, she stood before him. [13] And he said unto him, say now unto her, Behold, thou hast been careful for us with all this care; what is to be done for thee? wouldest thou be spoken for to the king, or to the captain of the host? And she answered, I dwell among mine own people. [14] And he said, What then is to be done for her? And Gehazi answered, verily she hath no child, and her husband is old. [15] And he said, Call her. And when he had called her, she stood in the door. [16] And he said, About this season, according to the time of life, thou shalt embrace a son. And she said, Nay, my lord, thou man of God, do not lie unto thine handmaid.

[17] And the woman conceived, and bare a son at that season that Elisha had said unto her, according to the time of life." (2 Kings 4:8-17 KJV).

Another case study of an act of kindness that birthed a different harvest is the experience of Tabitha in Acts of the Apostles chapter 9. Tabitha was committed to sewing coats and garments, and she would give them out to widows. Tabitha sewed clothes and sowed them into the lives of poor widows. When she died, those acts of kindness she did attracted harvest. Something in the spirit was stirred, not the blessings of clothing. Instead, God brought life back to her dead body, and she awoke.

"Now there was at Joppa a certain disciple named Tabitha, which by interpretation is called Dorcas: this woman was full of good works and alms deeds which she did. [37] And it came to pass in those days, that she was sick, and died: whom when they had washed, they laid her in an upper chamber. [38] And forasmuch as Lydda was nigh to Joppa, and the disciples had heard that Peter was there, they sent unto him two men, desiring him that he would not delay to come to them. [39] Then Peter arose and went with them. When he was come, they brought him into the upper chamber: and all the widows stood by him weeping, and shewing the coats and garments which Dorcas made, while she was with them. [40] But Peter put them all forth, and kneeled, and prayed; and turning him to the body said, Tabitha, arise. And she opened her eyes: and when she saw Peter, she sat up." (Acts 9:36-40 KJV).

Your goodness, acts of kindness, and generosity can be very potent. You cannot tell what they can bring forth for you in the future. Be confident that the good things you do will always come back to you; they will open doors of blessing you never imagined. Be a generous giver; make giving a way of life; and give consistently. Give whenever there is an opportunity to be a blessing. Give as an offering to honour God. Give to meet needs in the house of God. God honours these kinds of giving, and He will bless the giver. However, I'd like you to learn to place a demand on the Law of Harvest with your giving. Begin with intentional seed sowing, and when you make a seed giving, name the harvest you want, according to your heart's desires. Always declare what you are sowing your seed for and name the specific blessing you desire to come out of it as a harvest. When you declare or name your harvest, it will be noted in the spirit, and then you can expect it to happen for you.

There came a time in Abraham's life when God spoke to him and said He was going to bless him with a son. Furthermore, God said to Abraham that his descendants would be as numerous as the stars and that they would inherit the Canaan land. When Abraham inquired as to how he could be certain that what God said would occur, God instructed him to make a sacrifice.

> "But Abram said, "Sovereign Lord, how can I know that I will gain possession of it?" [9] So the Lord said to him, "Bring me a heifer, a goat and a ram, each three years old, along with a dove and a young pigeon." [10] Abram brought all these to him, cut them in two and arranged the halves opposite each other; the birds, however, he did not cut in half." (Genesis 15:8-10 NIV)

Know that there is always something you will have to sacrifice, sow, or give away to safeguard what is in the future. Today's sacrifice can pave the way for future glory. Today's pain can usher in joy tomorrow. Never hold back from giving away whatever you need to let go. It can birth something more and greater in the future.

Nine important things about seed time and Harvest

(a). There is the grace of God for giving.

There are many people who struggle with letting go. They hold firmly to their possessions. That attitude will only place a limitation on how much of God's blessings one can step into.

> "One person gives freely, yet gains even more; another withholds unduly, but comes to poverty. [25] A generous person will prosper; whoever refreshes others will be refreshed." (Proverbs 11:24-25 NIV).

When it comes to giving, a believer must understand that they do not give only because their personal needs have been met and there is a surplus. No! Believers are to give because giving is a Christian virtue. You must not be someone who is tied to material things. You must start giving at the level of generosity and walk your way into an abundance of supplies for all your needs (Philippians 4:18-19). You may need to receive the grace of giving to break the hold of materialism on you and become a generous giver. If you are having difficulty letting go of things you have acquired, even when you know you need to, pray and ask God for that grace. The giving grace was what the church in Macedonia had, such that they were pleading with Paul to accept their offering, and they gave exceedingly beyond what they themselves did not think they could do.

> "And now, brothers and sisters, we want you to know about the grace that God has given the Macedonian churches. [2] In the midst of a very severe trial, their overflowing joy and their extreme poverty welled up in rich generosity. [3] For I testify that they gave as much as they were able, and even beyond their ability. Entirely on their own, [4] they urgently pleaded with us for the privilege of sharing in this service to the Lord's people. [5] And they exceeded our expectations: They gave themselves first of all to the Lord, and then by the will of God also to us." (2 Corinthians 8:1-5 NIV)

There is the grace of God for giving. The church in Macedonia got it, and you too can have it. Ask the Lord for it today. It will allow you to let go of things that are important and valuable to you, but that you must let go of in order to gain access to what God has in store for you.

(b). Whatever God puts in your hand has both seed and bread.

> "Now he that ministereth seed to the sower both minister bread
> for your food, and multiply your seed sown, and increase the
> fruits of your righteousness;) 11Being enriched in everything
> to all bountifulness, which causeth through us thanksgiving
> to God". (2Corinthians 9: 10-11 KJV)

The bread is what you are to use of for your sustenance or to use to meet your own personal needs, and the seed is what you are to use to sow for tomorrow's harvest. You must start to see the seed in everything that you are blessed with by God, not only the bread. If you do not realise that there is both seed and bread in what you are given, and all you see is the bread, you are going to be consuming your seeds and forfeiting tomorrow's harvest. The seed is in everything you are given, so as you sow the seed, you can keep increasing until you reach the level of bountifulness.

> "But this I say, He which soweth sparingly shall reap also
> sparingly; and he which soweth bountifully shall reap also
> bountifully. [7] Every man according as he purposeth in his
> heart, so let him give; not grudgingly, or of necessity: for God
> loveth a cheerful giver. [8] And God is able to make all grace
> abound toward you; that ye, always having all sufficiency in
> all things, may abound to every good work." (2 Corinthians
> 9:6-8 KJV).

Make it a lifestyle that you are not going to consume all that God gives you, but that you are always going to purposely take out the seed first. Always take out the seeds before you finish them, no matter how small they are going to be. That is how you prepare for tomorrow. Understand that you do not start planting your seeds in the season you are meant to come into the harvest. You plant ahead so that when harvest time comes, you will have something. Many people do not understand this principle, so they initiate giving when they have come under some sort of difficulty, when that is the time, they should be praying for the manifestation of their harvest.

(c). **Your seed will determine your harvest.**

> "But this I say, He which soweth sparingly shall reap also sparingly; and he which soweth bountifully shall reap also bountifully. [7] Every man according as he purposeth in his heart, so let him give; not grudgingly, or of necessity: for God loveth a cheerful giver." (2 Corinthians 9:6-7 KJV)

You must have heard it said in church many times while referencing the scripture above that you should give as you intend it in your heart. What a lot of people do not realize is that they should arrive at that decision or purpose to give what they want only in view of the harvest they desire to have. Before you sow, you must decide in your heart what harvest you want. You are to be guided by the size of your desired harvest in your seed planting because not every size of seed can produce bountifully. If you decide for a bountiful harvest, you are to sow bountifully, but if you decide for a sparing harvest, then you are to sow sparingly. The kind of future you desire to have should guide your sowing principles. If you desire a breakthrough or for you to have the level of abundance that will take you out of all lack and obscurity, then you should not sow sparingly but bountifully. You cannot be a sparing sower and expect to reap a bountiful harvest. That is contrary to the law of sowing and reaping.

Many people have limited their giving, during the offering in church, to a certain amount and have stayed on that amount for years, wondering how come their harvest and increase have not been great and have remained the same for that many years. The answer is simple: increasing the number of seeds sown is the only way to increase harvest quantity. You are free to give as you decide. It is a choice that you must make. No one should compel you to do otherwise, and neither should you be sad about your decision. However, you must also appreciate the size of your harvest when it comes, as that is what you sowed for.

(d). Sowing sometimes requires a lot of courage

> "He that observeth the wind shall not sow; and he that regardeth the clouds shall not reap." (Ecclesiastes 11: 4 KJV)

It is not easy or comfortable to let go of something sometimes, especially when what must go is of significant value to the giver, or the time of the giving away is at a time when there is not enough to take care of all needs. As a giver, you must learn to sow by faith. Sowing by faith means one is simply following the Holy Spirit's lead in giving and is not minding his current circumstances. The best time to sow is when things are not going well and you desire to change the trajectory. You are to sow your way out of lack, struggles, and pain and into abundance and sufficiency.

It is easy to grow tired of giving for a variety of reasons, including a lack of funds, a plethora of other priorities, having given several times and seeing no results, and so on. Paying attention to these reasons is liken to a farmer observing the wind and being held down by it. If you are not stoppable from giving, I can assure you that it is only a matter of time before your harvest comes. Do not become wary of sowing, for whatever reason. Constantly be on the lookout for sowing opportunities.

> "And let us not be weary in well doing: for in due season we shall reap, if we faint not." (Galatians 6:9 KJV).

Beware that the times you are having challenges may be the toughest time for you to release the seed. However, they are also the best times to sow your seed. When your seed comes from a sacrifice, it appears to be more precious and valuable. The Bible says, "They that sow in tears shall reap in joy." (Psalms 126: 5 KJV). Seeds planted in tears are high-quality seeds, and they produce joyful harvest. The widow's offering in Mark 12 was commended by Jesus not because it was only two mites. Two mites is not a lot of money. Jesus was thrilled by her attitude toward giving and commended her because the two mites she put in the offering that day were all that she had. Jesus said of her offering that she made more sacrifice than the rich, who gave from their abundance and still had plenty left over.

> "Jesus sat down near the collection box in the Temple and watched as the crowds dropped in their money. Many rich people put in large amounts. [42] Then a poor widow came and dropped in two small coins. [43] Jesus called his disciples to him and said, "I tell you the truth, this poor widow has given more than all the others who are making contributions. [44] For they gave a tiny part of their surplus, but she, poor as she is, has given everything she had to live on." (Mark 12:41-44 NLT).

The Quantity of your seed matters and can impact the size of your harvest. However, the Quality of your seeds is more important than the quantity. A quality seed sown will always yield more than a large number of poor seeds. The sacrifice in the giving will determine the quality of the seed. The rich people in Mark 12 gave a lot more than what the widow gave. However, her mites were more precious to Jesus and had more worth because they came from a higher level of sacrifice. What the rich gave was a contribution. They were giving just to contribute to the storehouse. However, the widow was laying down her life by her giving.

(e). Giving must come out of the generosity of your heart.

Allowing your giving to come from the generosity of your heart is essential for God-like giving. And this is even more important when you are sowing into someone's life. One thing to always avoid doing is to treat God as a beggar or to use him as a money doubler, such that your giving is done selfishly, just for you to receive back what you gave in a greater measure.

> "Be not deceived; God is not mocked: for whatsoever a man soweth, that shall he also reap." (Galatians 6: 7 KJV)

You need to Underline <u>God is not mocked</u> in your Bible or highlight it on your device. God cannot be fooled. He sees and knows all things, even the hidden realities of our hearts. He always considers our motives, the thoughts of the heart, and His reward that will follow are determined by it.

> "Therefore, judge nothing before the time, until the Lord come, who both will bring to light the hidden things of darkness, and will make manifest the counsels of the hearts: and then shall every man have praise of God." (1 Corinthians 4:5 KJV)

There is no doubt that God rewards giving. However, He does not want our giving to be motivated only by the reward that we will receive. He wants us to be pure in heart and righteous in our motives—not selfish or greedy. You are not to be driven only by reward. You are to make your giving about honouring God, meeting important needs in people's lives, and helping solve the problem as well. Be driven and motivated by the change you are creating, the impact you are making with your giving, and always remembering Jesus's saying:

> "I have shewed you all things, how that so labouring ye ought to support the weak, and to remember the words of the Lord Jesus, how he said, it is more blessed to give than to receive." (Acts 20:35 KJV).

Here are the two things to keep to heart whenever you are giving to someone who is in need:

(I). Give from the generosity of the heart–this has to do with being able to give willingly, to the maximum, effortlessly, and without any expectation of receiving something back in return. Giving is powerful when you give to those who cannot pay you back.

> "The liberal soul shall be made fat: and he that watereth shall be watered also himself. (Proverbs 11: 25 KJV)

(II). Give out of the concern and the kindness of your heart. Develop a heart of compassion such that you will never see a need in someone's life that you can solve without doing anything about it. Ensure that your heart is not hard and that you are nonchalant towards people's pain. Allow what moves God to move you to action. Always pay attention to your heart when it is responding to a need and pulling you towards doing something about someone's predicament or pain.

> "He that hath pity upon the poor lendeth unto the LORD; and that which he hath given will he pay him again." (Proverbs 19: 17 KJV)

(f). Be aware that not every seed sown will fall on good grounds.

> "And he spake many things unto them in parables, saying, Behold, a sower went forth to sow; 4And when he sowed, some seeds fell by the way side, and the fowls came and devoured them up: 5Some fell upon stony places, where they had not much earth: and forthwith they sprung up, because they had no deepness of earth: 6And when the sun was up, they were scorched; and because they had no root, they withered away. 7And some fell among thorns; and the thorns sprung up, and choked them: 8But other fell into good ground, and brought forth fruit, some an hundredfold, some sixtyfold, some thirtyfold." (Matthew 13: 3-8 KJV).

There are some areas that will not support the growth of your seed. It is up to you to consider sowing seeds carefully. According to 1 Timothy 6:17–18, you are to be a liberal giver and, according to the Scriptures, you should always be ready to distribute and willing to communicate. However, it is important that you are also sensitive to God's prompting on when, where, and who to give to. Do not just give when you feel like it or when it is convenient for you. Learn to obey God and let go whenever he stirs you into giving. You will be planting in the wrong place if you are not sensitive and obedient to the leading of the Holy Spirit. The Holy Spirit is seeking to guide you always, even when it comes to your giving.

> "Thus, saith the Lord, thy Redeemer, the Holy One of Israel; I am the Lord thy God which teacheth thee to profit, which

leadeth thee by the way that thou shouldest go. [18] O that thou hadst hearkened to my commandments! then had thy peace been as a river, and thy righteousness as the waves of the sea:" (Isaiah 48:17-18 KJV).

God might want you to withhold giving to someone because he might use it on drugs that kill him while you're not looking. Sometimes the story that someone told you to get you to give to a course could be false and baseless, and if you give, it will be used for something completely different. Giving it to them will be like sowing a lie. It is good to be compassionate, but it is better to be God-led. Giving to the place or person the Holy Spirit is holding you back from giving to will turn into a waste, as it were. It is like sowing on stony ground. Whatever the case, being human means that we will all sometimes sow in areas that will not yield any harvest due to our limited knowledge.

(g). Learn to spread your seeds

"There is that scattereth, and yet increaseth; and there is that withholdeth more than is meet, but it tendeth to poverty. [25] The liberal soul shall be made fat: and he that watereth shall be watered also himself. [26] He that withholdeth corn, the people shall curse him: but blessing shall be upon the head of him that selleth it." (Proverbs 11:24-26 KJV)

You are not limiting your giving to a single location by spreading your seeds when you sow. This is another way of avoiding limiting your seed to grounds that are not good and will not produce any harvest for you. Moreover, your liberality is evident in the multiple ways you are giving, not just how much you are giving to that one person or one place. As you believe God provides multiple sources of income, you should also give in multiple ways and to various places. Learn to give just to be a blessing to someone, not necessarily to meet any needs in their lives, and learn to give to solve problems or take care of needs, wherever they confront you. Pay attention to give to the following:

- Give to honour people for who they are in your life
- Give as a sign of honour to your parents
- Give to support your pastors
- Give to those who labour in teaching and preaching the word in your church
- Give as a support to the poor
- Give to your church to help finance projects
- Give to fund the plant of new churches, not only the ones being initiated by your denomination
- Give to missionary organizations
- Give to missionaries and those who are serving in full time ministry.
- Give to the homeless on the streets of your city.

Don't just give to your church, don't just give to men of God, don't just give to members of your family. Also look for opportunities to bless people you've never met before, no matter who they are, where they come from, how they look, or what they believe. Here is what the Bible says:

> "And let us not be weary in well doing: for in due season we shall reap, if we faint not. [10] As we have therefore opportunity, let us do good unto all men, especially unto them who are of the household of faith." (Galatians 6:9-10 KJV).

The Bible says to do good to all men, not just a few, not only some people, or a particular set of people, but to all men. And to pay special attention to fellow believers, making certain that no one in the family of believers goes hungry.

(h). Do not only sow your seed, make sure you break your ground.

> "Sow to yourselves in righteousness, reap in mercy; break up your fallow ground: for it is time to seek the Lord, till he come and rain righteousness upon you. [13] Ye have plowed wickedness, ye have reaped iniquity; ye have eaten the fruit of

lies: because thou didst trust in thy way, in the multitude of thy mighty men." (Hosea 10:12-13 KJV).

For a believer, being the righteousness of God in Christ Jesus is not only a cliché. But it must also be the reality that he walks in. A believer must therefore consciously engage everything he does in line with the Word of God, in the fear of God, and in obedience to the leading of the Holy Spirit. Anything sown into the flesh—meaning contrary to and against the Spirit, will yield corruption. It will be ruined.

> "For he that soweth to his flesh shall of the flesh reap corruption; but he that soweth to the Spirit shall of the Spirit reap life everlasting" (Galatians 6:8 KJV).

The flesh represents the sinful nature of man. Therefore, sowing to the flesh would also mean doing something solely for self-gratification, which is contrary to God's word. Breaking your fallow ground means turning your land over so that what you plant can germinate, grow, and yield a harvest. When you plow, you get rid of the thorns, rocks, and all the things that will not allow your plant to grow, and you smooth the ground so the plant can grow in it nicely. The insight here is that you should not be sowing seed, believing the Lord for a good harvest, and yet you are engaging in things that are not right before Him, things that Satan can capitalize on to gain access to your domain and ruin your harvest. Take away from you and your affairs the things that will grieve the Holy Spirit and hinder Him from working out or bringing forth your harvest. It is one thing to sow, but it is another thing reap. The harvest is brought about by God. Paul the Apostle said:

> "I have planted, Apollos watered; but God gave the increase.
> [7] So then neither is he that planteth any thing, neither he that watereth; but God that giveth the increase." (1 Corinthians 3:6-7 KJV)

You may forfeit your harvest even though you are planting seeds if you do not honour God in your life and you keep doing things that grieve the Holy Spirit or even quench the Holy Spirit. If you let that happen, you are going to open the doors to the devourer, the caterpillars, and the cankerworms, and they will come in and eat up your harvest. Furthermore, the Bible says,

> "Take us the foxes, the little foxes, that spoil the vines: for our vines have tender grapes" (Song of Songs 2:15 KJV).

Never let your guard down and allow yourself to be swayed until you reach your harvest.

(i). Combine your giving with prayers.

Your prayer is like the rain that comes to water your seed. Keep praying, for by doing so, you are enabling your seeds to grow and mature. Giving and praying together can be very powerful. They can open the heavens for you, as Cornelius experienced:

> "He saw in a vision evidently about the ninth hour of the day an angel of God coming into him, and saying unto him, Cornelius. [4] And when he looked on him, he was afraid, and said, what is it, Lord? And he said unto him, thy prayers and thine alms are come up for a memorial before God." (Acts 10:3-4 KJV).

Do not sleep on your sown seed, pray over it until harvest. Prayer is not only like the rain that waters the plant, but it will also protect your harvest and ensure it becomes a reality. You have got to keep praying and speaking God's word over your seed and your harvest until you enter your harvest. Your prayers will make the ground too hot and unbearable for the caterpillars and the cankerworms. It will dry them up. Your prayers will drive away the little foxes that come to spoil the vine. Your continued Prayers will empower your ministering spirit in their warfare against your enemies. As in the case of Daniel (Daniel 26:36-46), they will keep fighting for you until the battle is won, and your harvest is delivered to you.

Chapter 4

BEWARE OF COVETOUSNESS

Covetousness can be a huge hindrance on the way to the fulfilment of God's promise of blessing in anyone's life. According to the Bible, one of the reasons some prayers are not answered is because of lust, which is a root cause of covetousness.

> "Ye ask, and receive not, because ye ask amiss, that ye may consume it upon your lusts (James 4:3 KJV).

Lust in the scripture above means a strong and uncontrollable desire for pleasure. This uncontrollable desire for things drives people to go to any length, sometimes unethically, to acquire material things. There are people who think having lots of material things makes them special, or that it would bring them satisfaction or make them feel complete. They think they are not complete without those material possessions.

Another word for covetousness is greed. It is the craving for everything good that one sees and doing everything to have it, even when it belongs to someone else. Furthermore, covetousness is the quality of tightly clutching what one has, even when it is intended to be given away. Being covetous means being uncontrollably drawn to material possessions, having an unhealthy desire for them, and clinging to them tightly. Covetousness usually stems from the false notion that a man's worth consists in the abundance of the things he possesses, which Jesus makes clear in his parable of the rich fool in the following passage of the Bible.

"And he said unto them, Take heed, and beware of covetousness: for a man's life consisteth not in the abundance of the things which he possesseth. [16] And he spake a parable unto them, saying, The ground of a certain rich man brought forth plentifully: [17] And he thought within himself, saying, What shall I do, because I have no room where to bestow my fruits? [18] And he said, this will I do: I will pull down my barns, and build greater; and there will I bestow all my fruits and my goods. [19] And I will say to my soul, Soul, thou hast much goods laid up for many years; take thine ease, eat, drink, and be merry. [20] But God said unto him, thou fool, this night thy soul shall be required of thee: then whose shall those things be, which thou hast provided? [21] So is he that layeth up treasure for himself, and is not rich toward God. [22] And he said unto his disciples, Therefore I say unto you, Take no thought for your life, what ye shall eat; neither for the body, what ye shall put on. [23] The life is more than meat, and the body is more than raiment." (Luke 12:15-23 KJV).

Jesus shares a parable in this passage and tells the sad story of a man whose farm yielded a bountiful harvest that year—the harvest was more than his storehouse could carry. Therefore, the rich man thought within himself and concluded that he was going to pull down the storehouse and build bigger ones that would have enough room to store the harvest. However, God killed him that night, before he could actualize his plans. God killed him that night, because he was not pleased with the rich man's decision. It is a tragic story.

Jesus shared this parable to pass the message about the harm covetousness can wreck in someone's life and to drive home the lesson that a man's life does not consist in the abundance of things that he possesses. The core of covetousness is that someone is laying up treasure for himself and is not rich toward God. Working to lay up treasures for yourself is a function of an accumulative spirit, the same spirit that is also behind idolatry. To have treasures and not be rich toward God implies that:

- the treasures that someone got have got influence over him.

- he is putting trust in his accumulated treasures to secure his future.
- the treasures he accumulated are there for his enjoyment and pride.
- the treasures are not being used to enrich God's kingdom here on earth.

No one should allow the acquisition of material things to be his sole motivation in life. No one should make material things the central thing about his well-being, his fulfilment in life, or happiness. No one should put his hope and confidence in his future based on what he has in his storage or bank account. Jesus regarded the above human behaviour as covetousness. God abhors covetousness:

> "For the wicked boasteth of his heart's desire, and blesseth the covetous, whom the Lord abhorreth." (Psalm 10:3 KJV)

To abhor means to despise or regard as abominations. God sees covetousness as equal to idolatry, which is an abomination before Him. God does not only abhor covetousness. He grades it at the same level and degree as idolatry.

> "For be sure of this: no immoral, impure, or greedy person-for that one is [in effect] an idolater-has any inheritance in the kingdom of Christ and God [for such a person places a higher value on something other than God]" (Ephesians 5:5 AMP)

An idolater is not only a person who has an idol or a grave image that he worships. He is also a person who has put material possessions at the centre of his life and will go to any length to acquire them.

The world grades people by their possessions and holds those who are in great possession of them as being highly valuable and esteemed above others, but it is not so with God. Even in today's churches, many people associate great wealth and material possessions with godliness. Wealthy people are given special seats in the pews. Wealthy young converts who do not know their left from their rights in the things of God are put on the pulpit to say something as a sign of recognition because they are wealthy. Prosperity has been elevated to a sign of godliness, so that many people in church today are showing off their prosperity as God's endorsement of them and their lifestyle. However, the possession of many good things in life is not proof of God's endorsement of one's lifestyle, nor is the increase in wealth and the acquisition of worldly goods indicative of godliness or proof of a closer walk with God. The Bible says, "...what does it profit a man if he gains the whole world [wealth, fame, success], and loses or forfeits himself?" (Luke 9:25 AMP). This means someone can be in possession of great wealth and yet be disconnected from God and be a lost soul. Indeed, as Jesus has said, a man's life does not consist in the abundance of the things that he possesses.

LESSONS FROM JESUS' LUKE 12 PARABLE

(a). There is nothing wrong with making an investment

There is nothing wrong with you farming, doing business, or making an investment in something to prosper. Jesus had no problem with the rich man's engagement in farming and growing fruits. God does not have any problem with us engaging in what will bring us profit. Instead, He desires that we keep being productive.

We have come to this understanding also by looking at Jesus' parable on the gift of talents in Matthew 25:14-29. In the parable, a certain master, who was embarking on a journey, distributed talents to his servants and instructed them to trade with them while he was away. However, the servant who received one talent did not engage in anything profitable with the talent he received.

> "So, I was afraid [to lose the talent], and I went and hid your talent in the ground. See, you have what is your own.' [26]
> "But his master answered him, 'You wicked, lazy servant, you knew that I reap [the harvest] where I did not sow and gather

where I did not scatter seed. [27] Then you ought to have put my money with the bankers, and at my return I would have received my money back with interest. [28] So take the talent away from him and give it to the one who has the ten talents" (Matthew 25:25-28 AMP).

We see that the master was displeased with the servant, who had one talent and refused to trade it for profit, and on account of that he was punished. The parable speaks of God's dealings with human beings. From the parable, we see that God is happy for you to go into investment and engage in things that will give you increase. It is also clear that God frowns on laziness and anyone's failure to engage in order to profit from or grow in their gifts.

(b). God is the God of increase

God does not only desire for you to invest and have an increase, but He also makes the increase happen. He is the God of increase, and He wants to give life and power to your investments and enable them to bring the desired increase. Paul the apostle said:

> "I have planted, Apollos watered; but God gave the increase. [7] So then neither is he that planteth anything, neither he that watereth; but God that giveth the increase." (1 Corinthians 3:6-7 KJV).

God does not only want you to increase, but He also finds it pleasurable when you are investing and are prospering.

> "Let them shout for joy, and be glad, that favour my righteous cause: yea, let them say continually, Let the Lord be magnified, which hath pleasure in the prosperity of his servant." (Psalm 35:27 KJV).

It is okay to start small. Moreover, most remarkable things start small. You must never despise a small start. However, God does not want you to stay small, where you started. He wishes for you to continue growing and expanding. The Bible says, "Though thy beginning was small, yet thy latter end should greatly increase" (Job 8:7 KJV). The increase is of God, and the lack of it is not of God. You must accept that God has no problem with anyone becoming rich or with any rich man becoming even richer.

The man in the parable was already rich, having storehouses, yet God blessed him with even more harvest than his storehouses could handle. God was not displeased with the rich man because his farm did very well. It was God who gave the increase, not the devil. You go ahead and seek it, invest in it, and work hard to achieve success. God is happy with it.

(c). Your worth is not measured by the material things you have acquired or accumulated

A lot of people who are into accumulating material possessions and hoarding them for themselves think that the things add to their worth. They look at their fat bank accounts, their expensive clothing, their fleets of cars, their jewerly, etc., and feel great about themselves. But as Solomon, who had great wealth, said, "They are all vanity of vanities" (Ecclesiastes chapter 1). By God's standard, material possessions do not add to your value, they are only tools giving to you, to serve in meeting human needs. Jesus clearly stated, "…Take heed, and beware of covetousness: for a man's life consisteth not in the abundance of the things which he possesseth" (Luke 12:15). Your worth is determined by how you use your wealth, the lives you touch with it, and the impact you make, not by how much you have saved up. You must realize that your worth is not determined by how much you acquire or accumulate here on earth. Your worth is measured by how much impact you make here on earth, particularly in people's lives, and by the contribution you are making to growing Jesus' kingdom here on earth. As you make use of your wealth to minister to the need of others, you lay for yourself treasures in heaven (1 Timothy 6:17-19). Your real value is in your heavenly treasure. You are worthless and living a meaningless life, as far as heaven is concerned, if all you are measuring is how much you have acquired and accumulated here on earth.

Everything you possess here on earth will vanish as vapour. You are not going to go to heaven with any of them. Their use is finished in this life. The irony is that there are many people who are like the rich fool in Jesus's parable. They are working so hard, acquiring wealth, and storing it up to be enjoyed in the future. They feel good beholding what they have acquired, and they feel good observing their fat bank accounts. It gives them a sense of worth and security because they have saved for their future, but sadly, they have no control whatsoever over the future. Many would die, just like the rich man in our story, whose life was taken the night he sat down and planned his future, and they would leave behind everything they worked extremely hard for, not having enjoyed the things they stored up for themselves. After they are gone, someone else will take over and squander everything they worked for in pleasure.

Do not let the accumulative spirit determine how you feel about yourself. Having so much does not make you more important. Begin enjoying life today with what you have, distribute it while you can, using what you have to touch as many people as possible and make a positive impact.

(d). God is not pleased when you show no regard for the purpose for which He gives increase

God does everything for a purpose. When God gives a man any increase, it is for a purpose. The first mistake this rich man made was thinking within himself about what to do with his bountiful harvest without seeking the will of God or his leadership on how to use the increase. The first thing a believer should do is acknowledge God in every circumstance and seek his will. You must remember that God is the one who makes your increase happen, and as a believer, you are to acknowledge Him first for every increase. You acknowledge God by honouring him with the first fruits of your increase.

> "Honour the Lord with thy substance, and with the firstfruits of all thine increase" (Proverbs 3:9 KJV).

Put God first in the equation before making your plans for how you will enjoy your increase. Deuteronomy 8:11-14 says:

> "Beware that thou forget not the Lord thy God, in not keeping his commandments, and his judgments, and his statutes, which I command thee this day: [12] Lest when thou hast eaten and art full, and hast built goodly houses, and dwelt therein; [13] And when thy herds and thy flocks multiply, and thy silver and thy gold is multiplied, and all that thou hast is multiplied; [14] Then thine heart be lifted up, and thou forget the Lord thy God, which brought thee forth out of the land of Egypt, from the house of bondage."

By forgetting God in your planning, you effectively attribute the glory for your increase to yourself, as if it came from your own strength and without God's intervention. If you believe that your increase comes from God, acknowledge Him for it, honour Him back, and seek His wisdom, which is the second thing a believer should do with every increase. Proverbs says Proverbs 3:7 "Be not wise in thine own eyes: fear the Lord and depart from evil." (KJV). It amounts to evil and foolishness to think you are wise by yourself and that you have what it takes to succeed without the help of God. Do not just consult your own thoughts. Seek God's wisdom on what to do with His blessings in your life, ask the Lord direction, and walk with Him, obeying what He says.

(e). God does not bring increase to meet only your own needs.

One of the reasons for you to consult God is because when you consult your own thoughts only, it is mostly going to end with me, mine, and I. The human mind is naturally self-centred and has the tendency to want everything for personal enjoyment and aggrandizement. God wants you to see every increase as God giving you a chance to be a source of blessing to someone. God always sees beyond one man, and He never does anything for anyone, so it can start and end with him. Paul the apostle reveals to us the mind of God toward the rich when he instructs Timothy to do the following:

"Charge them that are rich in this world, that they be not highminded, nor trust in uncertain riches, but in the living God, who giveth us richly all things to enjoy; [18] That they do good, that they be rich in good works, ready to distribute, willing to communicate; [19] Laying up in store for themselves a good foundation against the time to come, that they may lay hold on eternal life." (1 Timothy 6:17-19 KJV)

Do not get me wrong, there is absolutely nothing wrong with you personally enjoying your wealth. There is absolutely nothing wrong with using your wealth to live well, buy good clothes, live in good houses, drive good cars, go on vacation, etc. The Bible says in 1 Timothy 6:17 that God gives us richly all things to enjoy. God has no problem with your enjoyment. He wants you to enjoy living. He wants you to find genuine happiness and satisfaction in this life.

Your enjoyment is one of the reasons why God gave you the prosperity you have. However, your enjoyment is not the sole or the primary purpose for your prosperity. It is critical for a believer to understand that God does not bring increase solely for them to enjoy life. God moved Paul to tell Timothy to encourage the rich in the church to do good, saying that they are rich in good works, ready to distribute, and willing to communicate, laying a good foundation for themselves against the coming time. No believer should make living only about their enjoyment, but also about people and being a source of other people's happiness.

(f). Thinking only of yourself in your prosperity is covetousness.

From God's perspective, being covetous is not only when you want to take someone's own thing, but also when you possess so much and are only considering yourself in your plans for how you will use it, and you do not include anyone else in the plan. There is nothing wrong with desiring increase and praying to God about it. However, your motive in desiring to prosper is important to God. Your desire for more and intention to use all to meet only your own needs are covetous in the eyes of the Lord.

The rich man did not go after anyone's property, yet God sees him as being covetous. He invested well, worked hard for an increase, and God blessed his effort with a bountiful harvest. The Bible did not say that he stood in someone's way to obtain the increase, yet God called him covetous and foolish. Why is that? God regarded him as covetous because, in his pursuit of prosperity, all he considered in his plan was how he would spend his wealth solely on himself, with no regard for the poor and needy in his community.

You must always add someone as a co-beneficiary to the blessing of God in your life, and not only those within your family. One of the reasons why God is saying this to those who do not work to get a job or do something to make money is so that they too can have something to give.

> "Anyone who has been stealing must steal no longer, but must work, doing something useful with their own hands, that they may have something to share with those in need." (Ephesians 4:28 NIV).

Every believer must be involved in giving and receiving. It is not scriptural for a believer to use all the blessings of God only on himself. No matter how little, they must look for a way to get something from it and give to someone. Giving is a lifestyle that every believer must commit to. You must always look for opportunities to give something to someone and not only focus on your own needs and desires. When it comes to giving, a believer must understand that they are not to give only after all their needs are met or when they have surplus. No, you are to always look for opportunities to give because giving is a Christian virtue. The bible has a lot to say about giving. Consider the following scriptural references:

> "I have shewed you all things, how that so labouring ye ought to support the weak, and to remember the words of the Lord Jesus, how he said, it is more blessed to give than to receive." (Acts 20:35 KJV)

"Give, and it shall be given unto you; good measure, pressed down, and shaken together, and running over, shall men give into your bosom. For with the same measure that ye mete withal it shall be measured to you again." (Luke 6:38 KJV)

"One person gives freely, yet gains even more; another withholds unduly, but comes to poverty. [25] A generous person will prosper; whoever refreshes others will be refreshed." (Proverbs 11:24-25 NIV)

"There is that scattereth, and yet increaseth; and there is that withholdeth more than is meet, but it tendeth to poverty. [25] The liberal soul shall be made fat: and he that watereth shall be watered also himself." (Proverbs 11:24-25 KJV)

The church in Galatia understood the place of giving. They received the grace, and they operated under the grace. Therefore, they gave freely of their possessions and did not hold tightly to anything.

"And now, brothers and sisters, we want you to know about the grace that God has given the Macedonian churches. [2] In the midst of a very severe trial, their overflowing joy and their extreme poverty welled up in rich generosity. [3] For I testify that they gave as much as they were able, and even beyond their ability. Entirely on their own, [4] they urgently pleaded with us for the privilege of sharing in this service to the Lord's people. [5] And they exceeded our expectations: They gave themselves first of all to the Lord, and then by the will of God also to us." (2 Corinthians 8:1-5 NIV)

Even if you are in need, you should look for something you have that you can share with someone. Never live a life without giving. Only receiving and wanting more and not sharing is what the Bible refers to as covetousness. It is always better to give than to receive. In your giving, you will walk yourself out of lack and into abundance.

(g). God will not bring increase to make you at ease

Jesus said the rich man said to himself "and I will say to my soul, Soul, thou hast much goods laid up for many years; take thine ease, eat, drink, and be merry." (Luke 12:19 KJV). Wealth has the potential to make anyone feel at ease. To be at ease means to become confident and relaxed. Wealth can relax you to the point where you stop doing the things that brought you prosperity. You must never allow comfort to make you feel at ease because you will become vulnerable to the enemy, Satan.

Satan is hovering around constantly looking for an opportunity to devour you (1 Peter 5:8). The moment you let wealth and enjoyment make you relaxed, you will start to attract negative forces because they know you can become vulnerable when you are comfortable. The Bible says:

> "Woe to them that are at ease in Zion, and trust in the
> mountain of Samaria, which are named chief of the nations,
> to whom the house of Israel came" (Amos 6:1 KJV).

Although comfort can be a blessing, allowing it to make you feel at ease will put you in a situation where the spirit of the curse rules. Being at ease due to financial gain indicates that you have replaced your faith in the Lord with faith in wealth. Make sure that when the increase comes, you will not forget God. Make sure you do not become lukewarm in the things of God. Make sure that when the increase comes, you will not stop coming to church or become too comfortable to pray. Make sure you do not become too busy to have time to serve Him in the ministry you served in before your prosperity came. Make sure you do not become too important to evangelism.

Your attitude toward God, toward his work and people, must never change because wealth has come. You will hinder the blessing benefiting you and instead, you will attract curses, the negative forces behind misery, to flourish in your domain. As you increase in wealth, you must stay hot, ever-increasing in your passion for the things of God, keep working for God, volunteer in your church, keep being a blessing and give no room for apathy.

(h). God does not want anyone to make living all about enjoyment.

As I indicated earlier, one of the reasons why God blesses people with wealth is so that they can enjoy it. God has no problem with anyone enjoying life. You can buy any car you want; you can put on any clothes you want, you can go on exotic holidays, you can fly in a first-class cabin or even own a jet, God has no problem with all of that. The Bible says he gives us all things richly to enjoy.

> "Charge them that are rich in this world, that they be not highminded, nor trust in uncertain riches, but in the living God, who giveth us richly all things to enjoy" (1 Timothy 6:17 KJV)

However, God does not want anyone to make living all about enjoyment. Life is more than having things and enjoying them. You must not be a lover of pleasure, giving yourself to self-gratification and worldly desires (2 Timothy 3:1-4). You must have a sense of purpose. Your life must be more than just enjoying life. You must not devote your entire life only to acquiring material things for your enjoyment. That was one of the things about the rich man that God was not pleased with. He limited everything to enjoyment. He reacted to his newfound wealth by speaking to himself saying "thou hast much goods laid up for many years; take thine ease, eat, drink, and be merry" (Matthew 12:19). Your lifetime must mean more to you that having the good things of life and enjoyment them.

(I). God detests hoarding, it is a product of a covetous spirit

Simply put, hoarding is keeping something for yourself that you don't need or withholding more than is appropriate or justly due. Here is a scripture to support this:

> Proverbs 11:24 (AMPC)
>
> "There are those who [generously] scatter abroad, and yet increase more; there are those who withhold more than is fitting or what is justly due, but it results only in want."

God was not pleased with the rich man in Jesus' parable because all he wanted to do was break up his small storage and build bigger storage to keep every harvest his farm yielded for himself, and then relax for many years to come. He was intending on storing everything, including what he had no need for in the present, peradventure a future need arise. The Christian faith does not encourage grabbing. Instead, it encourages sharing. Unhealthy pursuit for wealth is greed, and hoarding, which is a fundamental aspect of the covetous spirit, is idolatry before God, and this is explicitly stated in the Bible: ".... Do not be greedy, for a greedy person is an idolater, worshiping the things of this world." (Colossians 3:5 NLT).

Many people, like the rich man, have continued to enlarge their bank accounts and save money for themselves that they will never need, and they are unconcerned about the situation of those around them, some of whom are in desperate need. Many people are expanding their wardrobes and are storing unused and old clothes, shoes, and bags that they have no need for and may never bring them out to wear. Hoarding is not only idolatry but also foolishness to God. God called this rich man foolish just for nursing the idea of hoarding. You need to break open your storage and get it cleaned up. Take out what you have stored over the years that you have no need for now. Do not keep enlarging your storage. Learn to give out whatever you have that you have no space for. You must not hoard what you have. That can be a life transforming blessing to someone.

YOUR MOTIVE FOR SEEKING PROSPERITY IS IMPORTANT TO GOD

I reconned that you picked this book and are reading it because the title resonates with you. I reconned, you desire to step into God's promises for you. I am glad you have this book. There are lots of promises in the Scriptures for believers, and you deserve to walk in the fullness of them. God desires that you experience His blessings far more than you desire that you do. However, understand that your motives matter to Him. Remember that God is the God of purpose. God can be held back from empowering you when your motives are misplaced. When you seek His prosperity, you must also answer the question of motive. Ask yourself, "What do you desire prosperity for? What would do you do with the breakthrough you are praying for? How would it affect you or the people around you if God changes your financial standing?" To do something about motive, you must start from your heart. The Bible says:

> "Keep thy heart with all diligence; for out of it are the issues of life" (Proverbs 4:23 KJV).

You must see to it that your heart is in a safe place with God. Ensure that your heart is right toward people and is not misplaced with respect to material possessions. Much of what happens in our lives is a result of what is going on in our hearts. The heart is the manufacturer of what happens in our everyday lives. The state of your heart is who you really are. Your heart's content is always going to be what you will become or produce outwardly. Before God picks someone up to use him for something significant, He first investigates the person's heart to see where it is in reference to God, people, and material possessions. If you desire God to show up in your life and prosper you, your heart must be right and pure.

> "Blessed are the pure in heart: for they shall see God" (Matthew 5:8 KJV).

The importance of the state of someone's heart when it comes to God choosing him for greatness was made clear when God sent a prophet to Jesse's house to pick one of his children as a replacement for Saul, the king of Israel (1 Samuel 16:7). The prophet Samuel was initially drawn to Eliab and Jesse's oldest son because he had a well-built physique and appeared physically fit for the throne. However, God rejected Eliab. God rejected Eliab because He was not pleased with what He saw when He looked at Eliab's heart.

> "When they arrived, Samuel noticed Eliab and said to himself, "Surely, here before the LORD stands his chosen king!" [7]

> But the LORD said to Samuel, "Don't be impressed by his appearance or his height, for I have rejected him. God does not view things the way men do. People look on the outward appearance, but the LORD looks at the heart."(1 Samuel 16:6-7 NET).

Human beings cannot see or read someone's heart, only God can. The rich man in our story in Luke Chapter 12 only thought within himself, but his thoughts sounded very loud before God. You can deceive people around you by impressing them with an outward show of piousness, but no one can deceive God, who searches the hearts of all men and knows the deep things of the heart. God always looks at the heart. He considers our motives and intentions before praising us for anything we do.

> "So then, do not judge anything before the time. Wait until the Lord comes. He will bring to light the hidden things of darkness and reveal the motives of hearts. Then each will receive recognition from God." (1 Corinthians 4:5 NET)

God gives praises only after He weighs the heart. He will answer your prayers only after He weighs your heart. He will make the increase you seek for, to come only after He weighs your heart. You must not be driven by lust (James 4:3). It will stand on the way of your prayer for increase. Free your heart from all forms of control (Matthew 22:37). Allow God's love to enthrall your heart. Let everything you do be motivated by your love for God and not by what you can gain materially. To defeat the spirit behind covetousness, you must make it a point of duty to always let go of anything that is starting to gain control over you. Never seek to have anything by hook or crook. Run away from anything that is not God, who is making the way for you to have it. It is not necessary to desire possessions in order to be equal to or better than others. Only keep what you know you can easily give away if you need to. Cultivate a giving spirit and use every opportunity you get to show someone a little kindness.

Chapter 5

REASONING TOGETHER WITH GOD IN PRAYER

The role of prayer in getting God's will manifested in your life or in any situation cannot be overemphasized. One of the ways we have the privilege of encountering God and experiencing His power is in the place of prayer. This privilege of having a conversation with God should be held in high regard in everyone's life because through it we can determine a lot of the things that can happen to us or in our affairs. Prayer is indeed an enormously powerful tool that God gave us. A believer must know how to pray and pray his needs into physical manifestation. Prayer is an immensely powerful tool that believers can use to get God to do amazing things. The following Bible reference says a lot about prayer potency:

> "Be careful for nothing; but in every thing by prayer and supplication with thanksgiving let your requests be made known unto God. [7] And the peace of God, which passeth all understanding, shall keep your hearts and minds through Christ Jesus." (Philippians 4:6-7 KJV).

No one should undermine the significance of prayer. It should be something we do constantly. The Bible does not only exhort that we pray constantly, but it also says to pray with all kinds of prayer:

"And pray in the Spirit on all occasions with all kinds of prayers and requests. With this in mind, be alert and always keep on praying for all the Lord's people." (Ephesians 6:18 NIV).

There are various types of prayers that we should be familiar with and actively engage in, such as thanksgiving prayer, intercession prayer, warfare prayer, declaration prayer, and confession of the word, among others. Another type of prayer you should use is reasoning with God. It is an extremely powerful type of prayer. Reasoning with God is another type of prayer of petition. Reasoning together with God in prayer is dealing with coming to God to rub minds, negotiate, plead your case, giving God reasons why He should answer you. It is important to Understand here that it is God Himself who makes the invitation for us to come and reason with Him.

"Come now, and let us reason together, saith the Lord: though your sins be as scarlet, they shall be as white as snow; though they be red like crimson, they shall be as wool." (Isaiah 1:18 KJV).

There are important things to be aware of when coming to reason with God. Here are some that I would like you to take note of.

YOU MUST APPROACH GOD WITH FULL AWARENESS THAT HE IS A FATHER.

The most excellent way to approach God is as your father. Coming to God as you would a father makes all the difference in reasoning together with God in prayer. Jesus taught us to see God as a father whenever we come to Him. Jesus says, "After this manner therefore pray ye: Our Father which art in heaven, Hallowed be thy name" (Matthew 6:9 KJV). Seeing God as a father and approaching Him with that understanding is critical in your ability to reason with Him. How you will approach a father is going to be different from how you will approach your boss or a judge. The relationship between the president with his son is different from what exists with his staffers. In the sight of a son whose father is the president, he is more a father who happens to be president. He talks to the father freely, with confidence, as son to a father and not as son to the president. You are freer before a father no matter how highly placed, he is in the society, and no matter how powerful or wealthy he is. This is so because you know that father cares, you have his attention, he is your present help when in need, someone you rub minds with, and he will protect you.

A son gets away with what someone who is not the president's son dears not. You will be able to reason with God if God is not only the Almighty, a judge, and a consuming fire God to you, but also your Heavenly Father. And you know that you have the care and attention, as well as the protection of your father, and that makes a whole lot of difference. The premise of the son-and-father relationship gives power to reasoning with God's prayer and allows it to flourish. It is only in this light that the believer derives the boldness required for reasoning with God in prayer. Jesus wants the believer to approach God as a father because of the boldness it brings to the believer. Your prayer life will revolutionize once you start approaching God as your father. If you can see that He is your father, Psalms 103:13-14 will start to make a lot of sense to you and will give you a son-like boldness before Him. Hear what the scripture says:

> "Like as a father pitieth his children, so the Lord pitieth them that fear him. [14] For he knoweth our frame; he remembereth that we are dust." (Psalm 103:13-14 KJV).

Matthew puts the caring nature of Father God into a powerful way. He says, "If you, then, though you are evil, know how to give good gifts to your children, how much more will your Father in heaven give good gifts to those who ask him" (Matthew 7:11 NIV). This is to assure you that Father God, cares about your needs and concerns, that He is ready and willing to listen to your prayers, and that He will withhold nothing good from you.

YOU ARE TO APPROACH GOD WITH FULL ASSURANCE OF HIS ACCEPTANCE

God does not want us to come to Him feeling guilty and unworthy of His presence, but to come with confidence, feeling righteous and accepted by God.

> "Let us therefore come boldly unto the throne of grace, that we may obtain mercy, and find grace to help in time of need" (Hebrews 4:16 KJV).

Having the full assurance of being accepted by God and the assurance of His love and care will give you the boldness you need to engage God without feeling unworthy or undeserving of His blessings. You need this boldness in reasoning with God. Moreover, we are admonished in the scripture to approach God with boldness.

> "Having therefore, brethren, boldness to enter into the holiest by the blood of Jesus, [20] By a new and living way, which he hath consecrated for us, through the veil, that is to say, his flesh; [21] And having an high priest over the house of God; [22] Let us draw near with a true heart in full assurance of faith, having our hearts sprinkled from an evil conscience, and our bodies washed with pure water." (Hebrews 10:19-22 KJV).

Boldness is derived from the knowledge that a pathway into the holiest place, the very presence of Father God, has been created and consecrated for us by the blood of Jesus. Boldness is derived from the knowledge that we have a high priest, Christ Jesus, and that He is also the surety of our eternal salvation, guaranteeing our continual access to the father and access to our rights and privileges as sons of God. Armed with this understanding, all believers have the right to come to God. The sense of unworthiness and lack of qualified or guaranteed acceptance in God's presence is an evil conscience that we must overcome. We must learn to be confident in approaching God and have no need to be afraid to express ourselves before Him because He is a caring father.

> "Give all your worries and cares to God, for he cares about you." (1 Peter 5:7 NLT).

> "However, those the Father has given me will come to me, and I will never reject them." (John 6:37 NLT).

You must understand that God cares about you and that there is nothing that can happen or that you will do that will make Him reject you. As a believer, it is important you understand that you do not come to God feeling like a sinner, in need of forgiveness, and you go praying "please Lord, forgive me for any sin I have committed, even sins that I am not aware of." Coming to God and feeling that way is being sin conscious; it is an evil conscience. In Christ Jesus you are forgiven completely, of every sin (Ephesians 4:32; Colossians 1:14). In Christ Jesus God has nothing against you (Colossians 2:13-14; Roman 5:18; Ephesians 2:15-22). In Christ Jesus God does not go about following you and watching to catch you on every sin to punish you for it. God does not even go monitoring unbelievers and lying-in wait to catch them so that He will punish them, not to talk of those who have been redeemed by the blood of Jesus. Watch the following scripture:

> "Therefore, if any man be in Christ, he is a new creature: old things are passed away; behold, all things are become new. [18] And all things are of God, who hath reconciled us to himself by Jesus Christ, and hath given to us the ministry of reconciliation; [19] To wit, that God was in Christ, reconciling the world unto himself, not imputing their trespasses unto them; and hath committed unto us the word of reconciliation." (2 Corinthians 5:17-19 KJV)

God is in the business of reconciling the world to himself, not imputing trespasses to people. On account of the death of Jesus, every human being is forgiven, and those who have made Him Lord and saviour have received it, the forgiveness. Do not be sin conscious such that anytime you come to pray you are saying Lord please forgive me of any sin that I might have committed, knowingly or unknowingly. In the Christian faith the confession of sin should not be done abstractly or vaguely. You cannot say "Lord please forgive me of anything you have against me that I am not aware of. "That is being sin conscious. Believers are to be righteousness conscious. Instead come before God saying, "Thank you Lord for making me right before you in Christ Jesus." "I am grateful I have right standing with you." (Romans 3:21-26; 2 Corinthians 5:21). A confession of sin is an admission of wrongdoing. You must have known that you had committed the sin. You are to own up to it, name it, and be sorry about it, whilst acknowledging that forgiveness has already been given in Christ Jesus.

Someone will say, "what about the sins that I am committing that I am not aware of"? You do not need to worry about that, it will be sin conscious to be worrying about something you think you did but you have no knowledge of. God does not go about imputing their trespasses" (2 Corinthians 5:19). Nothing is being counted against anyone if he is not aware that what he does is sinful. Sin is knowing what you should do and refusing to do so. The Bible says, "remember, it is sin to know what you ought to do and then not do it." (James 4:17 NLT). It is not a sin if you are not aware it is. Moreover, as believers, we have the Holy Spirit on the inside of us. The Holy Spirit on the inside of the believer will guide them into all truth and remind them of what God said (John 14:16-18, 26; John 16:13-15). It is the responsibility of the Holy Spirit to let the believer know whenever he has strayed and done something that God is not happy about. The Holy Spirit will always convict the believer whenever he goes contrary to God's Word.

When you sin, you will know it if you have the Holy Spirit inside of you. He will make sure you know it so that you will do it right and not give Satan an opportunity in your life. If He does not convict you, then whatever you thought was a sin was not. Furthermore, another good reason a believer should not worry about sins that he might have committed but is not aware of it, is because the blood of Jesus is constantly cleansing the believer from all sins, even sins that he is not aware of, sin he will not be able to acknowledge, since he does not know they exist. God has put a system in place for the continues purification and sanctification of believers, so that believers will not live in guilt, going about worrying, fearful, and having a feeling of unworthiness.

> "But if we walk in the light, as he is in the light, we have fellowship one with another, and the blood of Jesus Christ his Son cleanseth us from all sin." (1 John 1:7 KJV)

When we come together in fellowship in the presence of God during a congregational gathering of believers, the Holy Spirit effectively cleanses and sanctifies every believer. This is the process through which God is perfecting believers and qualifying them.

> "But ye are come unto mount Sion, and unto the city of the living God, the heavenly Jerusalem, and to an innumerable company of angels, [23] To the general assembly and church of the firstborn, which are written in heaven, and to God the Judge of all, and to the spirits of just men made perfect, [24] And to Jesus the mediator of the new covenant, and to the blood of sprinkling, that speaketh better things than that of Abel" (Hebrews 12:22-24 KJV).

This is why anyone who is a believer must not forsake the assembling together of believers (Hebrews 10:25). In the general assembly, there is the blood of sprinkling, which is constantly speaking good things over them, and the perfection of believers' souls is being implemented.

REASONING WITH GOD ON THE GROUND OF HIS WORD AND PROMISES.

The platform on which you can reason with God is only the basis and strength of His word. God is only committed to His word; His word is His bond, and He watches over it to perform it.

> "The Lord said to me, "You have seen correctly, for I am watching to see that my word is fulfilled" (Jeremiah 1:12 NIV).

God's promises are yes and amen. They are grounded, and they happen. The word God spoke cannot return to God void, and not having accomplish what He spoke it for.

> "So shall my word be that goeth forth out of my mouth: it shall not return unto me void, but it shall accomplish that which I please, and it shall prosper in the thing whereto I sent it" (Isaiah 55:11 KJV).

The promise of God is the ground on which reasoning, together with God in prayer, stands. Armed with the understanding of the reality of the immutability of God's promises provides you with the platform to stand on and reason with God. In your reasoning, you tell God what His word says about your request or the situation you care about and seek His intervention. Reasoning together with God in prayer, was the prayer Moses prayed when God said to Him that He would destroy the whole people of Israel and start a new nation with Moses (Exodus 32:7-14). The people of Israel had left Egypt and arrived at Sinai. At Sinai, God called Moses to come up to Mount Sinai. He was going to give Moses the commandments that would regulate the relationship that would exist between God and the people of Israel. Moses was on the mountain with God for forty days and when the people saw that Moses had stayed long on the mountain, they feared that Moses died, so they made for themselves a golden calf and worshiped it, attributing to it the glory for their deliverance from Egypt.

God was enraged with the people, and He planned to wipe them off the face of the earth, replacing them with a new generation of people led by Moses. Moses knew what the word of God said concerning Israel. He knew of all the promises that God made to their fathers, to Abraham, Isaac, and Jacob. Armed with this understanding, Moses stood in the way of God by contending and reasoning in prayer with God. He requested that God reconsider His decision and change His mind. Moses had the guts to tell God to relent, repent, or have a change of mind. Moses referred to what God thought of doing as evil and a disaster. The Bible says Moses said to God:

> "Why should the Egyptians say, 'It was with evil intent that he brought them out, to kill them in the mountains and to wipe them off the face of the earth'? Turn from your fierce anger; relent and do not bring disaster on your people" (Exodus 32:12 NIV).

Moses could reason with God in this manner because he knew his position with God, he had access to God, and he spoke to God face to face (Exodus 33:11). Moses understood God's regard for him; it was close to God's heart, and this understanding gave him the confidence to speak freely. Furthermore, Moses knew that God was a covenant keeper, merciful, and compassionate. You need to study Moses' line of reasoning with God in Exodus 32:7-14, and you will be amazed at his intercessory prowess and the great courage with which he reasoned with God. Indeed, it takes a man who knows his covenant position and his place in the heart of God to speak in that manner. The Bible says we have a better covenant established upon a better promise than what Moses had.

> "But in fact the ministry Jesus has received is as superior to theirs as the covenant of which he is mediator is superior to the old one, since the new covenant is established on better promises" (Hebrews 8:6 NIV).

What we have with God in the new covenant is superior to what God had with Moses and the people of Israel. They had not experienced redemption. They were not born again. They did not have the Holy Spirit living on the inside of them. They had not become the righteousness of God in Christ Jesus, the pathway into the holiest was not consecrated for them, they had no high priest who was sitting at the right hand of God and making intercession for them, guaranteeing their eternal salvation. The New Testament believers are extremely fortunate. We can approach

God with boldness, armed with His word, plead our case. You can come to God to reason with Him, Telling God who you are in Christ Jesus, what His Word says concerning you, and reminding Him of His promises. God is delighted for you to recall what He has done or said to Him.

> "I, even I, am he who blots out your transgressions, for my own sake, and remembers your sins no more. [26] Review the past for me, let us argue the matter together; state the case for your innocence (Isaiah 43:25-26 NIV).

Your ability to come to God, Standing on His word, and promises, to pray and plead your case is the most powerful way to pray. You lock your mind with God's mind, and reasoning with God's line of reasoning when you are referring His word to Him. I present to you that this indeed is the most potent way to pray. The Bible says,

> "And this is the confidence (the assurance, the privilege of boldness) which we have in Him: [we are sure] that if we ask anything (make any request) according to His will (in agreement with His own plan), He listens to and hears us" (1 John 5:14 AMPC).

God is not committed nor is He obligated to listen to any prayer that is not lining up with His will, and therefore Jesus said to pray "your will be done on earth" (Matthew 6:10 KJV). Arming yourself with the understanding of God's will and replaying it back to Him; that is reasoning with God. He hears and He answers prayers prayed this way.

REASON WITH GOD BY PUTTING A DEMAND ON THE LAW OF HARVEST

This aspect of reasoning with God works on the basis of the understanding that God is a rewarder. The rewarder nature of God is the very core of our relationship with Him, and the foundation on which our faith must be grounded. There are two fundamental things on which our faith must be established upon, based on Hebrews 11:6. This verse of the scripture says, "But without faith it is impossible to please him: for he, that cometh to God must believe that he is, and that he is a rewarder of them that diligently seek him." (Hebrews 11:6 KJV).

The two things about faith from the scripture above are:

- **Believe that God is** -

  Faith is acknowledging and resting on the revelation of God as we have been given in the scripture. God is not who you think, God is who the Bible says He is; the acceptance of that is faith. The Bible says God is immortal, invisible, and only wise, the creator of all things, deliverer, the provider, the healer, the miracle worker, the one who holds tomorrow, the one who does not change, the one whose counsel is immutable, etc. You must believe that He is Who He says He is, and He must be that God to you personally.

- **Believe that God is a rewarder** -

  The other aspect of faith is acknowledging that God is a rewarder. He cannot, not reward. Rewarding people is His nature, not rewarding is antithetical to God. It will amount to God being unrighteous to forget one's labour of love and not reward it. The Bible says, "For God is not unrighteous to forget your work and labour of love, which ye have shewed toward his name, in that ye have ministered to the saints, and do minister." (Hebrews 6:10 KJV). He surely pays believers for every virtuous deed, and the reward is not only when we get to heaven. No, Jesus says the reward starts in this life.

  "And Jesus answered and said, Verily I say unto you, There is no man that hath left house, or brethren, or sisters, or father, or mother, or wife, or children, or lands, for my sake, and

71

the gospel's, [30] But he shall receive an hundredfold now in this time, houses, and brethren, and sisters, and mothers, and children, and lands, with persecutions; and in the world to come eternal life." (Mark 10:29-30 KJV).

The rewarder nature of God is another solid ground on which you can reason together with God in prayer. The idea is that you can come to God armed with your honourable deeds and seed sown and place a demand on your harvest. This was the type of prayer King Hezekiah approached God with when he was told by Isaiah the prophet that he was going to die. King Hezekiah fell ill, and it was unto death, for God had sent Isaiah the prophet to tell him to put his house in order because he was going to die and will not live.

"In those days was Hezekiah sick unto death. And the prophet Isaiah the son of Amoz came to him, and said unto him, Thus saith the Lord, set thine house in order; for thou shalt die, and not live. [2] Then he turned his face to the wall, and prayed unto the Lord, saying, [3] I beseech thee, O Lord, remember now how I have walked before thee in truth and with a perfect heart, and have done that which is good in thy sight. And Hezekiah wept sore. [4] And it came to pass, afore Isaiah was gone out into the middle court, that the word of the Lord came to him, saying, [5] Turn again, and tell Hezekiah the captain of my people, Thus saith the Lord, the God of David thy father, I have heard thy prayer, I have seen thy tears: behold, I will heal thee: on the third day thou shalt go up unto the house of the Lord. [6] And I will add unto thy days fifteen years; and I will deliver thee and this city out of the hand of the king of Assyria; and I will defend this city for mine own sake, and for my servant David's sake." (2 Kings 20:1-6 KJV).

Hezekiah's experience with God taught him that God is a rewarder, and because he did not want to die, he reasoned with God, asking Him to remember his service and good works. It was recorded that when Hezekiah heard what the prophet said, he turned his face to the wall and prayed unto the Lord, saying, "Lord, remember how I have walked before you in truth and with a perfect heart, and remember how I have done what is good in thy sight." Hezekiah was saying to God, "This is not how to reward someone who has pleased you." You should not pay him with death but with life instead. God heard him, changed His mind, and restored life to Hezekiah. God was quick to hear Hezekiah, such that even while the prophet Isaiah was still in the king's court and on his way out, the Lord told him to turn back and prophesy differently to Hezekiah the King. God did not only increase King Hezekiah years by fifteen more years. He also added protection and deliverance to the reward. The law of harvest is immensely powerful. Hezekiah invoked it in prayer, and withdrew from his store of harvest, life, deliverance, and protection when he was faced with death.

You deserve to reap what you sow. And you can come to God armed with your good works, asking for Him to consider them and bless you. Today, ask the Lord to remember your sown seeds and all your sacrifices. Go ahead and plead your case. I pray Psalms 20:1-4 over you right now!

> "May the Lord answer you in the day of trouble! May the name of the God of Jacob set you up on high [and defend you]; [2] Send you help from the sanctuary and support, refresh, and strengthen you from Zion; [3] Remember all your offerings and accept your burnt sacrifice. Selah [pause, and think of that]! [4] May He grant you according to your heart's desire and fulfill all your plans" (AMPC)

Chapter 6

INHERIT YOUR PROMISE THROUGH FAITH AND PATIENCE

It's one thing to know God's promises for you, too fast and pray about them, and to have a seed of faith in them, but it's quite another to be able to actualize them. Faith and patience are an important must have for everyone, especially in their season of waiting, for them to receive the physical reality of what they prayed for and are anticipating from God. Watch the following scripture:

> "We do not want you to become lazy, but to imitate those who through faith and patience inherit what has been promised" (Hebrews 6:12 NIV).

This scripture above shows us how the people who were before us inherited the promises that God made to them. The scripture says they were not lazy, but they actively applied FAITH and PATIENCE, and as a result, they received or inherited the promise of God. Working out Faith and patience is challenging work, which is why the Bible in Hebrews 6:12 says not to be lazy. If you are waiting on the Lord for something and desire its manifestation in the physical, you must understand faith and patience and the role they play in birthing realities. Faith and patience go hand in hand to bring to make God's promises a reality. Wherever you see faith, it produces patience, and wherever you see patience, it is being sustained by faith. Applying faith and patience will require you to actively do something. I like to show you how faith and patience work and what to do with them.

FAITH - YOUR LINK TO THE SUPERNATURAL

The first thing to be aware of is that your faith is important in your relationship with God. It will determine the quality of your relationship with God, and how much you can enjoy the blessings of the kingdom of Jesus (Hebrews 10:38). Your faith is an important part of your journey toward the things God has promised you. If you don't take care of your faith and let it grow, you'll end up with nothing special.

Another thing to be aware of is that without faith it will be impossible for you to please God (Hebrews 11:6). The believer is made right before God only by faith; he can never be right before God outside of faith. So as a believer, you must live by faith, through and through (Hebrews 10: 38). One of the two things about faith in Hebrews 6:12 that we also considered in the previous chapter was that faith entails believing that God is. God is who the Bible says he is, not what you think, or who someone else says he is. The knowledge you have about God must not be affected by any circumstance. No matter where you are, no matter your experience, no matter what you are seeing or hearing, you must maintain your belief that God is… a healer, the one who blesses, the one who delivers, the one who makes increase happen, the who creates, the miracle worker, He calls the things that are not and they appear, etc. Never doubt the power and ability of God. Faith is to hold your understanding of Him and what He says firmly, knowing that no matter how long His word tarries, God's word will eventually happen and not return to God as void.

HOPE DEFERS MAKES THE HEART SICK

When the thing that you are hoping for seems very distant and there is no physical evidence that you are making progress towards its actualization, you are likely to feel as you are only chasing shadows, or as if you are on the road to nowhere (Proverbs 13: 12). This feeling can be frustrating and can lead to despondency. Does this resonate with you? We all sometimes go through challenging times and experiences. Things do not always work out as we expect them to. We experience delays, we suffer defeat, and life can become hard and tough. At such times, we may feel like life is not fair, wondering where God is in all of it. This tough and challenging season is called "trying times." It can be a very trying time when things are going wrong for you and you have no answer for them. It can be a trying time when what you hoped for tarries and people are saying that it is because you committed a sin, that you are faithless, that you are not doing some things right, or that you are not praying enough. However, that may not be the case. It may not be about not praying enough or not walking right with God. It may have something to do with timing, meaning THAT it is not yet God's timing for your breakthrough. Whatever the case, we may not fully understand why some things happened the way they did. The scripture says our knowledge is partial and incomplete.

> "Now our knowledge is partial and incomplete, and even the gift of prophecy reveals only part of the whole picture" (1 Corinthians 13:9 NLT).

There are certain things for which we are not going to have answers on this side until we see Jesus face to face. Your faith must be based on the finished work of Christ. In the midst of your difficult experience, you may have low moments. However, believe that what God's word says is done, and that what God promised will be fulfilled in your life And have it at the back of your mind that trials of faith are a season for you to prove your faith in God and your confidence in His word. The situation may have arisen, orchestrated by Satan, to challenge your conviction about the word of God and to check how firmly you are standing in your relationship with God. It is a time for you to stand firm, be unmovable and abound in the work of the Lord, because you know that your labour is not in vain in his sight.

> "Therefore, my dear brothers and sisters, stand firm. Let nothing move you. Always give yourselves fully to the work of the Lord, because you know that your labor in the Lord is not in vain" (1 Corinthians 15:58 NIV).

You must understand that delays and trials are sometimes a pointer to a great destiny ahead. Your miracle may be taking time to give you time to mature and be ready for what is coming. Most big and tall trees take their time growing downward, underground, before surfacing above the ground for all to see. All of the women in the Bible who experienced a delay in conception, such as Sarah, Isaac's mother, Rebecca, Jacob's mother, Rachel, Joseph's mother, Samson's mother and his father, Manoah, Hanna, Samuel's mother, and even John the Baptist's mother and father, Zachariah, all gave birth to great people. Satan wants you to forfeit God's promises for you by making you walk away, turning back from the things you hold dear and have trusted God for. Satan knows that the delaying season can be trying for you, he knows that it is a potential season for you to lose hope. As such, he will turn up the heat on you but do not let go, whatever the case may be. Hold tied to what you believe. Continue to walk in faith, never turning back.

> "But we are not of them who draw back unto perdition; but of them that believe to the saving of the soul" (Hebrews 10:39 KJV)

There are two extremely important aspects of faith that you must understand and live by. These are OBEDIENCE OF FAITH and FAITH LOVE. I consider the obedience of faith and faith love as the operating vehicles which faith delivers through. Without the obedience of faith and faith love, faith is ineffective, and powerless. You are going to need obedience and love to empower your faith and produce your desired results.

(1). Obedience of faith

Faith is more than just how you think or speak. Your thoughts and words have an impact on your faith walk. However, faith demands that you do more than think positively and speak in line with the word of God. You must add obedient actions to it. It is critical that you understand what God is telling you to do at each stage of your journey to where you want to go. And you must follow His instructions. You must always remember that faith is more than just accepting that what God says is so and declaring it. You must know God's instructions for you and how the Holy Spirit is leading you to act, and you must obey Him for your faith to be powerful and creative. Your faith will be meaningless, a dead faith, and powerless, if it is not accompanied by obedience to the leading of God. The scripture says,

> "But now is made manifest, and by the scriptures of the prophets, according to the commandment of the everlasting God, made known to all nations for the obedience of faith" (Romans 16:26 KJV).

It is through the obedience of faith that the scripture comes alive and the fruits of salvation are manifested. The word of Prophecy of the scripture does not manifest until the obedience of faith is given to it. The lack of regard FOR and obedience to God's word, can be the cause of delays in the fulfilment of God's promises. Jesus is committed to enforcing everything that comes with your salvation. However, that is also dependent upon your obedience to him. Jesus is not committed to your prosperity, nor is He under obligation to make happen for you all the things you are laying claim to as the by-product of your salvation until you obey Him. For the Bible says, "And being made perfect, he became the author of eternal salvation unto all them that obey him" (Hebrews 5:9 KJV). You must never be in that place where you are believing God for a miracle and yet you are living in disobedience to His word.

You must be ready to do whatever God says. He will speak to you in a manner and at a level that you will understand. He will speak to you through the word as you sit down to study it. He will speak to you through visions, dreams, and revelations. He will speak to you through the messages from the pulpit. You need a word from God to get you out of some trouble in life. The word of God will come to you to get you out and to move you forward. Make sure you are not disobedient to what God is speaking to you about.

> "Then they cry unto the LORD in their trouble, and he saveth them out of their distresses. 20He sent his word, and healed them, and delivered them from their destructions" (Psalms 107: 19-20).

Sometimes people get stuck in life and don't make any progress or have a significant breakthrough because God is speaking to them but they aren't listening. What God says to do may not make much sense. Nonetheless, you must learn to obey Him. His word to you is your saving grace. You should consider doing obedience check-ups from time to time to ensure that you are not disobedient in any aspect. When there is a delay or something you prayed for did not work out as you hoped, you should do an obedience check-up to ensure yourself that it is not due to any disobedience on your part. Self-examination is what God says to do (1 Corinthians 11:28; 2 Corinthians 24:5).

(2). Faith love –

Your faith needs love to function unhindered. Faith expresses itself through love. Whilst Obedience can be likened to a car engine, Love is as the engine lubricant, or the engine oil. As a car without an engine is only a container, so is any faith that does not have obedience. Also, as an engine being driven without engine oil will knock, so is faith that is lacking in love and not able to express itself. Love lubricates faith, enabling it to perform wonders without inhibition. Your obedience to God's word and your love walk will make your faith very explosive.

"For in Christ Jesus neither circumcision nor uncircumcision
avails anything, but faith working through love." (Galatians
5:6 (NKJV)

Your faith needs love to be expressive, potent, creative, and result oriented.
You must be filled, consumed, driven, and motivated by love in all the
things you do. Protect your love for God, protect your love for people,
and look for ways to demonstrate them to make your faith work for you.
Bible states expressly in Romans 5:5 that our hope is guaranteed to not
fail and would come to be if our hearts are filled with God's love.

"And hope does not put us to shame, because God's love has
been poured out into our hearts through the Holy Spirit, who
has been given to us" (Romans 5:5 NIV)

You must make up your mind to love people irrespective of what they
do or say about you. Make the decision that an offense will not interfere
with your love walk, no matter who the offender is. Satan is always going
to try to stand in the way of your miracle by stirring people up and
making them offend you, and this will occur mostly during the period
when Satan senses something good is about to come to you. People will
do or say nasty things to you for no reason. Satan will use people to
sow bitterness in you, keep you in pain, and force you to fight back.
He knows that if he can get you to abandon your love walk and act in
disobedience to God's word by harboring malice and hatred for people,
he can render your faith ineffective. The Spirit that you have inside of
you is the Spirit of love:

"For God hath not given us the spirit of fear; but of power, and
of love, and of a sound mind" (2 Timothy 1:7 KJV).

The spirit that you carry is the capacity to love anyone, irrespective of
who they are, where they come from, what they do, or how they live their
lives. Hating people is no longer in your DNA as a child of God because
of the spirit that you have inside you. You go ahead and show the love
of God to all the people around you, whoever they are. People may do

you harm, but you cannot do them harm in any form. People may take advantage of you, but you cannot take advantage of anyone. The love of God shed abroad in you (Romans 5:5) is the ability to see good in all people, it is the ability to accept, relate, tolerate, bear with, and work well with people, irrespective of what they stand for. The spirit of love inside you is the ability to not harm people, no matter what they do. You must not do any harm to anyone, but love.

The spirit of love inside you is the power to do good, both to friends and to people who have treated you as their adversary (Romans 12:21). You must get rid of all bitterness, offer forgiveness, and let all offenses go. Move your love higher up. The more you are offended, do not lower it down. I assure you that as you move your love higher, such that there is no one person you cannot love or forgive, you are going to start to see God's power working in you and through you, as you have never experienced it before, and you will start to see and enjoy more victories.

PATIENCE - THE POWER IN YOU TO WAIT IN HOPE

This chapter on faith and patience is especially important if you are believing in God and waiting for a breakthrough. In life, the believer will encounter oppositions, contend with adversaries, and go through all sorts of trials of faith. In the midst of all that, he must fare through, with patience to reach his destiny. Here are somethings about patience to keep at heart. (a). Patience is the ability to wait for something for as long as it will take without worrying or complaining. (b). Patience is the capacity to tolerate the pain of delays. (c). Patience is the wherewithal to hold back from doing something stupid or destructive in your waiting season. (d). Patience is the power that enables you to hold your ground and keep expecting what you hope for, even when there are no physical indicators to hold on to.

Patience is necessary for you to reach your harvest season. It is necessary because, by experience, we know that God does everything in his own time, not ours. Therefore, we also know that certain things that we desire to have may not come at the time we want them, and we will have to wait for God's timing, which may be longer than we want. If you have no patience, you are going to jump out of the waiting mode and ruin things. It is understandable that it is not easy to wait, especially for the things you needed as of yesterday, but then, you are not God. None of us is, and there are things and situations you have no control over, so, you will need to wait on God's timing to have them. In your time of waiting, you will be tempted to change focus and try something else. Changing your focus and direction may appear to be the wisest thing to do. However, if you believe that God's promises are yes and amen and that what you were focusing on is His promise for you, then you must hang in there and wait for it, despite the temptation to change course.

> "For ye have need of patience, that, after ye have done the will of God, ye might receive the promise. [37] For yet a little while, and he that shall come will come, and will not tarry" (Hebrews 10:36-37 KJV)

In the time of your waiting, understanding the worth of the thing you are waiting for and giving it the value it deserves are vital. Anything that is precious to you will be worth waiting for. When you patiently wait for something, the longer it takes, the more you demonstrate that you understand the value of the item and how much it means to you. Know that anything you put value in, you will attract, and if you wait for it, though it may take a little while, it will eventually show up for you. These two things are critical to patience:

(1). Doing the will of God - Do not forget that one of the things about patience is that it is the ability to wait for something for as long as it will take without worrying or complaining. What you do during the waiting period is important. You cannot fold your hands and do nothing. You cannot afford to become depressed, disillusioned, secluded, or locked up away from people. You cannot afford to be carried away with doing things just to keep busy, even when the things you are doing have no bearing on your destiny. While you await your breakthrough, it is important to figure out the things God is assigning you to do during the waiting period. Staying within His will and purpose for you is what will hasten your miracle.

> "For ye have need of patience, that, after ye have done the will of God, ye might receive the promise. [37] For yet a little while, and he that shall come will come, and will not tarry" (Hebrews 10:36-37 KJV).

Determine what it is that God wants you to do. Search your heart, and He will reveal it to you. It matters and is relevant to the fulfilment of what He is working out for you. You will lose a lot if you don't mind and do what God wants you to do. But as you stay in His will, He will hasten the manifestation of what you are waiting for. Even if you are unhappy in your marriage, God's will may be for you to stay in it. God's will may be for you to stay in the job and not accept the other offer, even though it does not pay much. God's will may be for you to remain in the city and not leave, even if all doors are closed. God's will may be for you to keep going and seeking reconciliation with her, even though you have gone a few times and she will not budge. God's will may be for you to remain in that church and keep serving in the ministry He called you to serve, even though your team members seem not to like you and no one appreciates your gift. God's will may be for you to keep sowing that seed, even though you have not seen any harvest yet.

If you can figure out God's will, you have got to engage it until He says otherwise, and He will make His word good in your life. I assure you that as long as you are obedient and stay within God's will. He will, in turn, ensure that He brings good things to you. For the Bible says, "If ye be willing and obedient, ye shall eat the good of the land" (Isaiah 1:19 KJV). Do not say, "I am patiently waiting on God," because then you are going about living your life and not being mindful of what God wants for you. Understand that anytime you step out of God's will, you will open your life and destiny to the devil, who is the enemy of your success and happiness. You have no guarantee of safety or a guarantee of God's protection when you step out of His will and plan for you.

No matter how long the delay lingers, keep attending congregational worship, keep serving in your church, keep praying, keep giving, keep loving, and keep sharing the gospel. Become acutely aware of the leading of the Holy Spirit and obey Him, even when what He is saying to you does not make much sense. It is okay. Sometimes, what God instructs us to do does make any sense to the human mind. It does not make any sense to turn the other cheek when someone hits you on the other. Neither does it make sense to give someone your shirt when he forcefully takes your coat. However, that's God's way of doing things (Luke 2:29). Always remember that your obedience is extremely critical to walking in faith.

(2). **Patient-endurance:** Anything involving endurance speaks of hardship, pain, difficulty, or challenges. By "patient endurance," I am saying that there could be pain involved in the waiting season, and it can be difficult, such that if you cannot add endurance, you are going to jettison what is being processed for you and is on the verge of manifestation. I have seen in many situations that delays can really be tough and painful. A couple who married a few years ago and planned to start a family right away but have yet to conceive can understand the agony of infertility. A young woman who is getting older and closer to menopause, who is not married but wants to start and raise a family, can understand the pain of the delay.

In talking and praying with many young people who graduated from university but do not have meaningful employment years after graduation, I could feel their frustration and pain. As a pastor, I have had people ask me what was wrong with them and whether they were under any curse because of the pain and sometimes the embarrassing comments of others about their situation. It can even become more frustrating and painful when delays drag and family and friends are asking all kinds of questions and making all manner of suggestions, insinuating that something is off about you. You can understand this if you have ever found yourself in a helpless situation before. That was the sort of situation Abraham had to endure.

Try to picture it in your mind. Abraham was very wealthy but without an heir, and the culture he lived in was the kind that put great emphasis on the necessity for a man to have male child who is to be the heir, a descendant, or a progeny who is to continue the family line. Having an heir was so important to them that it could lead to either divorce or polygamy. The pressure on Abraham was enormous. Also imagine what went on in Sarah's mind. In their time, women's roles were primarily to give birth to children and to raise them. Women who were unable to conceive were thought to be barren; it was believed that God had closed their wombs due to some sin or a curse.

These women suffered stigma and shame. A good example of such women who had to endure such shame was Hanna, the wife of Elkanah, in 1 Samuel1:6-10. It must have been such a challenging and enduring season of waiting for Father Abraham and Sarah his wife. Though Abraham's experience was a challenging one, it ended beautifully. Abraham obtained the promise, and Sarah, his wife, gave birth to Isaac, his son. Hallelujah!

> "For when God made promise to Abraham because he could swear by no greater, he sware by himself, [14] Saying, Surely blessing I will bless thee, and multiplying I will multiply thee. [15] And so, after he had patiently endured, he obtained the promise" (Hebrews 6:13-15 KJV).

God did for Abraham as He promised, and Sarah, in her old age of 90 years, received power, conceived, and gave Abraham a son, Isaac. The promise of God for Abraham came through because the Bible said that Abraham, "......after he had patiently endured, he obtained the promise" (Hebrews 6:15). Patient endurance is a critical factor in your waiting season. Waiting can be difficult because you will be bombarded with all kinds of opinions and suggestions. Some people, out of care and concern, though erroneously, will counsel you to reconsider your stand. They will tell you to take a second wife to have a child. They will tell you to secretly sleep with someone, commit adultery, and have a baby. They will tell you that it is foolish not to compromise your position and accept the bribe in order for you to prosper because life has been difficult for you. They will tell you God did not speak to you about the vision you shared, and they will seek to redirect you.

However, do not allow your waiting and the things you suffer as a result to make you put a stop to what God is already working out for you. You have no control over the things that will bombard you in your waiting season, and you cannot determine how long the process will last. However, the onus is on you to maintain your position and stay the course. Patient endurance means you must choose to cope with whatever the waiting season unleashes. You must decide to continue hoping and confidently holding on to God's word, not wavering. In closing this chapter, I would like you to pay attention to the following scripture:

> "Cast not away therefore your confidence, which hath great recompence of reward. [36] For ye have need of patience, that, after ye have done the will of God, ye might receive the promise" (Hebrews 10:35-36 KJV).

Chapter 7

RECOGNIZING YOUR OPEN DOORS

A n open door is when God removes a barrier or a limit that is in the way of someone and he is granted access to a new experience, a new place, or a new height. An open door comes in diverse forms. An open door can be in the form of a new opportunity given to someone for him to do something new or a rare chance for him to achieve something significant. An open door can be a new season of increase someone is ushered into, such that he is experiencing amazing growth without much effort, or having to do anything different from what he did prior to the opening of the door. An open door can appear as a sudden breakthrough given to someone against a physical or spiritual barrier, launching him into a new realm of goodwill, favor, or a new dimension of success or wealth.

An open door can come in the form of an invitation to a new place where it was not expected or a rare opportunity to meet someone, and the contact with the person has the potential to be life-changing. Open doors can also be referred to as a gateway, a chance, or an opportunity. When God opened a great door for Paul at Ephesus, it was a door of fruitful ministry, and his ministry flourished there, so much so that many people accepted Jesus as their Lord, and many churches were birthed during this time. The Apostle Paul wrote:

"For a great door and effectual is opened unto me, and there
are many adversaries." (1 Corinthians 16:9 KJV)

God opens doors for people to create a space for them to find expression
for their gifts, to have new opportunities, to meet new people–the people
that are relevant and connected to their destiny–and for them to succeed
and prosper. Any new day is a potential day for you to have an open
door that can usher you into a new season of your life, for you to have
a brand-new experience, and for you to achieve new success. God works
with times and seasons to execute His plan and move people into their
destinies.

"To every thing there is a season, and a time to every purpose
under the heaven" (Ecclesiastes 3:1 KJV).

Nothing happens randomly with God. God is purposeful, intentional,
and timely. He has set a time and season for everything in human affairs.
God has plans for you, in God's plans for you, He intends that you will
become somebody and achieve something significant in your lifetime. A
particular number of days has also been earmarked for you to live here on
earth, you will exit the scene when those number of days are complete.
The number of days you have been given to live on Earth is made up of
times and seasons of life. The times and the seasons are designed for you
to use for your growth, formation, and fulfilment. In order words, times
and seasons are for you to function in, to become all that is in God's plan
for you. Within the amount of time, you are given to live, God will create
for you open doors at various stages.

Every new day, you must be on the lookout for an open door in all seasons
of life. You never know when and cannot tell at what season or time a
door will open for you, and unless you are expecting it, it will come and
expire without you realising it. I pray that a door will not open for you
and you will miss it.

BE AWARE OF YOUR TIME AND CHANCES IN YOUR SEASON OF LIFE

What distinguishes between some successful people and failures, poor people and wealthy people is the understanding of their gift of time and chance. Time and chance are given to all men, irrespective of their strength, wisdom, skills, talent, or even their spirituality. The Bible says that the race you are to run, the battles you must fight and win, the wealth you are to create in this life, and the favour you are to attract, are all packaged within time and chance.

> "I returned, and saw under the sun, that the race is not to the swift, nor the battle to the strong, neither yet bread to the wise, nor yet riches to men of understanding, nor yet favour to men of skill; but time and chance happeneth to them all" (Ecclesiastes 9:11 KJV).

You will lose if you do not know how to use your time, or recognize your chance. You must understand that there is no one person that God is in enmity with. He does not stand in the way of anyone's success, simply because the people have no relationship with Jesus. The Bible says He makes the sun shine upon both the evil and the good, and He sends down the rain upon the farm of both the evil and the good (Matthew 5:45). God will create a chance for everyone, and anyone who uses it effectively will prosper. If you look around, you would see many people who have no relationship with Jesus, but have achieved overwhelming success, and are very wealthy. They achieved their success because God creates chances for everyone.

An Open door for a breakthrough or for someone to achieve a great exploit happens within the gifts of time and chance. Many successful people are not any different from the rest of the people. They only recognized their open doors and used their time well. On the other hand, many highly gifted and talented people will end up as mediocre, having accomplished nothing significant in life, and may die poor. These many people who may finish underachieving, and may die poor will do so not because they lacked the ability to achieve greatness, but because they do not understand the gifts of time and chance. You must realize that a fundamental key to being successful is understanding timing and your chances in life.

TIME AND TIMING MATTER FOR ACHIEVING DESTINY

Time is the season of your life, packaged in minutes, hours, and days. Every minute of your time is precious and matters to your destiny. Timing is the point or period when something needs to be done. It is that space in time you are required to perform. You must become aware of time and its value and never misuse the time of your life. Always have it at the back of your mind that there are number of days allotted to you here on earth. It is the time of your life, and you will not be here forever. Time gone is part of your life gone, and equally, time wasted is part of your life wasted. You must learn how to redeem your time, as we are admonished in Ephesians 5:16 and Colossians 5:5. Redeeming your time is about using your time wisely, effectively, fruitfully, and beneficially, and ensuring that your time is never wasted. However, if peradventure, you wasted your four hours of time yesterday, in redeeming your time, you are to look for a way to payback that time by doubling your effort today and putting in more time today in the area you lost time yesterday.

On the other hand, to redeem time also means that you may ask the Lord for the anointing of speed, so you may achieve in a fleeting time what would have taken you a longer time to achieve. A good example of the anointing for speed is the experience Elijah the prophet had when the hand of the Lord came upon him, and he ran and overtook Ehab's chariot (1 Kings 18:45-46). You must become aware of the timing for doing something. Timing is critical because in God's way of doing things, at your set time, He releases grace, favour, and He pulls the necessary things together for you—things that you will need to get something done. You may find something difficult and frustrating if you get into something

90

before your set time. Things may not work out for you then, not because they are not meant to, but because you went in ahead of your time, at a time when the grace for it was not released.

A good example of what I mean is the story about Moses. Moses injured himself and ended up in exile on the outskirts of a desert because he wanted to be the deliverer before his appointed time.

> "And it came to pass in those days, when Moses was grown, that he went out unto his brethren, and looked on their burdens: and he spied an Egyptian smiting an Hebrew, one of his brethren. [12] And he looked this way and that way, and when he saw that there was no man, he slew the Egyptian, and hid him in the sand. [13] And when he went out the second day, behold, two men of the Hebrews strove together: and he said to him that did the wrong, Wherefore smitest thou thy fellow? [14] And he said, Who made thee a prince and a judge over us? intendest thou to kill me, as thou killedst the Egyptian? And Moses feared, and said, surely this thing is known. [15] Now when Pharaoh heard this thing, he sought to slay Moses. But Moses fled from the face of Pharaoh, and dwelt in the land of Midian: and he sat down by a well." (Exodus 2:11-15 KJV).

Moses was born to be Israel's deliverer. However, he needed God to open the door to his calling for him. The door will naturally open at the set time. Moses, on the other hand, did not wait for the appointed time; he desired to use His earthly royal position and physical strength to be Israel's deliverer, but he was rejected by the people he was born to deliver (Exodus 2:23-25; Exodus 3:1-4). When it is your time, God will open a door for you, and you will achieve results without much effort. Never forget that timing is important in utilizing the grace of God, going in too soon may make you suffer untold hardship and pain unnecessarily.

As you become more aware of the value of time and timing, you must eliminate time wasters. Procrastination is one of the time wasters to eliminate. Procrastination is a thief of time, learn to defeat it wherever it confronts you. Take care of what you need to take care of today, do not push it till tomorrow. Two things can happen when you procrastinate. Firstly, you will be receiving the grace of God in vain. The Bible says to not receive the grace of God in Vain:

"We then, as workers together with him, beseech you also that ye receive not the grace of God in vain. [2] (For he saith, I have heard thee in a time accepted, and in the day of salvation have I succoured thee: behold, now is the accepted time; behold, now is the day of salvation" (2 Corinthians 6:1-2 KJV).

Now that this is settled, when the time comes for you to engage in something, which God has also opened a door for you to do, God will pour out the grace that will enable you to be effective in it. That grace will be wasted and received in vain when you procrastinate and do not step in to get it done. The second thing that can happen when you procrastinate is that the time you waste may have eaten up a good chunk of the amount of time you have left to accomplish the task before you, and you may not have sufficient time to complete it. A good example on this is the story of Joshua, Moses' successor. Joshua became distressed and discouraged after Moses died. He was so engrossed and overwhelmed by Moses' death that he became disheartened and failed to arise and lead the people God chose him to lead. God had to jolt Joshua into action by announcing to him again that Moses was dead and emphasizing that Joshua cannot keep reminiscing over their past with Moses, and he must arise and go forward.

"Now after the death of Moses the servant of the Lord it came to pass, that the Lord spake unto Joshua the son of Nun, Moses' minister, saying, [2] Moses my servant is dead; now therefore arise, go over this Jordan, thou, and all this people, unto the land which I do give to them, even to the children of Israel" (Joshua 1:1-2 KJV).

The time that Joshua wasted, though short, meant so much to them in achieving their destiny. Joshua did well and accomplished many feats for

Israel. However, when he was old and his time on earth was coming to an end, he realized there was much more he could have accomplished.

> "Now Joshua was old and stricken in years; and the Lord said unto him, Thou art old and stricken in years, and there remaineth yet very much land to be possessed" (Joshua 13:1 KJV).

You must maximize every time, every moment, and every opportunity given to you to do something and kill procrastination. Otherwise, you are going to wake up one morning, and realize that do not have much time left to achieve what is before you. One important principle of life is to learn to do what you need to do today because you may not get another opportunity to do it. You must be acutely aware of timing and always remember that time spent is time gone. Any time that passes is gone, you will never have it back. Furthermore, if you do not do what you are meant to do at a set time, you may never get the time to do it again. There are certain things that you can only do effectively in your youthful days. If you do not utilize those times, you may not be able to get around them in your old age. That is why the Bible says:

> "Remember now thy Creator in the days of thy youth, while the evil days come not, nor the years draw nigh, when thou shalt say, I have no pleasure in them" (Ecclesiastes 12:1 KJV).

AN OPEN DOOR IS YOUR CHANCE WITHIN TIME

Remember that at various stages within your lifetime here on earth, God will create for you a chance. Remember that time and chance are God's gift to all people (Ecclesiastes 9:11). Do not forget that a chance is also an open door or an opportunity. If you can spot your chance, not miss it, and use it effectively, you will progress steadily until you reach your full potential. God created the opportunity for Moses to encounter Him by putting before him the burning bush scene. Moses responded to the bush opportunity in a positive manner, for he said, "...I will go over and see this strange sight—why the bush does not burn up" (Exodus 3:3 NIV). Moses would have missed the opportunity had he walked away, ignoring the burning bush. But he encountered God, and it changed his entire life because he did not miss the chance. The Bible says, "When the Lord saw that he had gone over to look, God called to him from within the bush, "Moses! Moses!" And Moses said, "Here I am." (Exodus 3:4 NIV).

Every day and throughout their lives, God gives everyone a chance. Chances are created to help change your life and bring you into your destiny. Chances will help take you to a place where your destiny is connected. Chances will bring you into contact with people that have something to do with your destiny. Chances will give you a forum that is exceedingly rare for you to display your gift. When you can see an open door or a chance and you can seize the moment and grab it, utilizing it effectively, things will change for you. You must learn to give a second look to whatever your spirit is drawn to. Do not just walk away until you can confirm for certain that it is not 'God's door' for you. There are chances for you to lookout for, and not let them pass when they present themselves to you. Chances such as:

- **The opportunity to train and develop yourself.**

  Training and developing yourself continually is critical for your maturity and ability to receive certain blessings from God. If you ignore training and your personal development, a chance may open for you to move up in life, to get a better paid role, or go into partnership with certain class of people, but you may not be qualified for it, and will forfeit it.

- **The opportunity to invest for financial empowerment.**

  You must always be on the lookout for an investment opportunity. They will present themselves to you, take the risk, overcome your fears. You never can tell whether it is a wonderful opportunity or not till you try it. Do not live your life and always wish you had tried something.

- **The Opportunity to make a new friend.**

Few years ago, God told me to put value on relationships. He told me, "Musa, everybody needs somebody. There is a place you may never go to until someone takes you there. There is something you need to know but may never figure it out until someone shows it to you. There is someone you need to meet, meeting the person will change your life for good, but you may never meet the person until someone introduces you to him. You need people. You must put value on relationships."

- **Opportunity to be a blessing to someone.**

You never can tell the person you are helping today may be the destiny helper that you are going to need tomorrow. The Bible says, "Be not forgetful to entertain strangers: for thereby some have entertained angels unawares" (Hebrews 13:2 KJV). Who you help today could be the angel you going to need in the future.

- **The Opportunity to travel.**

Something that you need may not be located where you are based, God will have to move you out of your base for you to find them.

- **The Opportunity to sow a seed.**

An opportunity given to you to sow a seed is only a setup to position you for a harvest. You will forfeit that level of sufficiency if you ignore the chance given to you to sow. Never overlook a chance to sow a seed. The Bible says,

"In the morning sow thy seed, and in the evening withhold not thine hand: for thou knowest not whether shall prosper, either this or that, or whether they both shall be alike good." (Ecclesiastes 11:6 KJV).

NOT EVERY CHANCE IS AN OPEN DOOR FROM GOD

Always be prepared for opportunities to present themselves. God will see to it that they do so throughout your life. However, you must also realize that not all opportunities that present themselves will be from God. You must understand that simply because something seems right, looks attractive, and is readily available to you, that does not mean that it is from God. The Bible says,

> "There is a way that seemeth right unto a man, but the end thereof are the ways of death." (Proverbs 16:25 KJV)

Before you access any open door, try to know the source of it. Satan also creates opportunities for people to deviate from their destiny, harm them, cause them to suffer losses, or waste their valuable time. Time wasters in particular are a powerful tool used by Satan. Satan can open a door for you to become a millionaire, but he is only using the door to keep you away from God's door, which will make you a billionaire. And by the time you realize it, you would have put in several years at the place. Do not spend your time 'succeeding," in what is not part of your destiny. It is mediocrity, the success can never be measured in comparison to the success you could have had in your destined location.

Do not jump into anything simply because it looks attractive. It may appear attractive, but it may not be what God wants for you. Avoid investing your precious time in something that you may have to walk back from and start all over again. You can never get back the time you have given to it. I say to young people, whenever I get the chance, not to go into a relationship or marriage simply because the person asking for their hand in marriage is a nice person, is good looking, or simply because it has been a long time someone asked them out, and they do not want to miss this person, thinking, they do not know when another person would show up. Being a nice person does not make anyone a great spouse. Always take your time to pray about it before you accept anything offered to you. Do not give your precious time to someone who will waste it. It is your life.

GOD DOES SHUT SOME DOORS DOWN

God does not only open doors, but He also shuts down doors too. So, you must understand that not all closed doors are the handiwork of Satan.

> "To the angel of the church in Philadelphia write: These are the words of him who is holy and true, who holds the key of David. What he opens no one can shut, and what he shuts no one can open" (Revelation 3:7 NIV).

Yes, God shuts some doors. However, God never shuts doors against anyone to subject him to a life of pain and misery. God is a good God; He only does what is good and perfect (James 1:17). Sometimes, God needs to close certain doors to make you see what He has been seeking to draw your attention to. He closes doors that are not a blessing to you. If they are not closed, you may be ruined. Before you stick to any door, that is closed against you, and praying, and fasting for it to be opened, you need to find out whether it was God who closed it or not. Closed doors may come in different forms or shapes. A closed door could be the end of a relationship that is a waste of your time and resources, and is damaging to your health, and well-being. The relationship was never meant for you. It is not going to work, and there is nothing you can do about it. You have put so much into it, and you still are doing a lot to see it restored, but it is like flogging a dead horse, nothing good will come out of it, it will only cause you more pain. Cut your losses, accept the reality, and let go. Nothing must be a do or die thing for you. Learn to let go what you must, when you should. Do not insist on what God is not making happen for you.

A closed door could also be the end of a job or an existing business deal. God may be seeking to move you higher, give you your own company, and link you up with new partners, and it will take you to a greater success, but you do not see it. Sometimes God closes a door in a place because you have overstayed in the place, He has been seeking to move you forward, but you do not see it, so he jettisoned what you are counting on, so that He will take you out and move you up. The Bible says, "But he brought us out from there to bring us in and give us the land he promised on oath to our ancestors" (Deuteronomy 6:23 NIV). There are places or jobs that people overstay in, and they will not leave until they are pushed out. They do not leave, even when it is obvious that there is no more goodwill there. They will not leave because they feel secured or are feeling guilty about leaving, as though they will be betraying their employer. Some will not leave for fear of uncertainty, fear of leaving their comfort zone, fear of the new, fear of the unknown, for job security, etc. Sometimes people get fired, and God is behind it. He does that to move them up.

A closed door could also come in the form of a quit notice to vacate your house, and God let that happen so you can move on to purchase your own house. Whenever a door is closed against you, do not be hasty in breaking it down. Look closely, God could be in it.

RECOGNISING THE DOORS THAT GOD OPENS

When God opens a door for you, it stays open until you discover it. You may miss them, and it may seem like they are lost, but they stay open until God Himself closes them, no one else can close them, not you, not Satan, not anyone, only God can. The Bible says, ".... what he opens no one can shut, and what he shuts no one can open" (Revelation 3:7 NIV). Satan can only stand in your way, resist your advancement, distract you, and take your attention away from the direction you should go, or make you blind so you cannot see the doorway before you, but He cannot close the door that God has opened. I pray for everyone reading this book, who missed an opportunity or fail to recognize an open door, that God will redeem the time for you, meaning, may God take you in full circle, with great speed, and help you to rediscover your rightful place and take it. May God reorder your steps and bring you back to where you should be, in the mighty name of Jesus.

You must begin to value any opportunity that keeps coming your way, any offer that keeps coming your way and staring you down, even if you keep passing it up. The door that is opened by God stays open until He closes it. Take a peek the next time it presents itself. It could be a 'God door.' An important aspect of the doors that God opens, is the fact that, it will not require you to compromise your values to access it. Absolutely, it will not be a 'God door,' if it requires you to compromise your standing with God. Another important aspect of a door that God opens is that it will not cause harm to you or your family. If it is harmful to your health, your marriage, or harmful to your family, and it takes you away from your service to God, it cannot be a 'God door.' An open door from God may sometimes appear to be bigger than what you can handle, however, the resources you need to take it on, and make it successful will be made available to you, and it will not cause you stress. Any door that God opens will be a great and effectual door.

> "For a great door and effectual is opened unto me, and there
> are many adversaries." (1 Corinthians 16:9 KJV).

A great and effectual door means that when you go through the door and grab the opportunity it presents, it will transform your life, it will bring you success, it will move you higher in life, it will turn you into a blessing, and you will be an impactful blessing. God will only open doors that will lead you to glory rather than shame. It is not a great and effective door if no significant change is observed about you after you enter it. And there are losses instead. Whatever the case, know that any time God is doing something new and life-changing in you or for you, it will attract adversaries. Satan does not go to sleep because good things are happening to you. That is nothing new, it happened to Paul, for he said, "…great door and effectual is opened unto me, and there are many adversaries." (1 Corinthians 16:9 KJV).

The presence of a challenge, opposition, or difficulty is not indicative of the absence of God there. Great and effectual doors attract adversaries, but here is the point, they cannot close the door that God opened, and they cannot stop your shine. The subsequent and last chapter of this book deals with being aware of the enemies of your progress. Do not jump and go there yet, continue reading. There are vital things I would like you to grasp before I draw this chapter to a close.

YOU NEED GOD TO HELP YOU SEE AN OPEN DOOR

It is quite possible for someone to stand before an open door and not recognize it. I am sure you have heard people saying, "if I knew I would have married him or her and not let go." "If I knew, I would have invested in the company, I did not know their shares will double in such a short period." "If I knew I would have accepted the offer, I did not know that what I had will collapse" etc. An opportunity can present itself to you, and you could miss it unless God opens your eyes to see it. You need God to open your eyes for you to see and recognize an open door. The story of Hagar readily comes to mind here.

It happened that Hagar fled from Abraham's house because Sarah, her master, was hard on her. Hagar took her son Ismael with her and fled. When they arrived in the desert, their water had run out, and the boy cried because he was very thirsty, so that Hagar was afraid, he would die. She took the boy and put him under the shrubs and departed a distance away because she could not watch him die. Unknown to Hagar, there was a well of water within the vicinity. However, she could not see it until God opened her eyes to see it.

> "God heard the boy crying, and the angel of God called to Hagar from heaven and said to her, "What is the matter, Hagar? Do not be afraid; God has heard the boy crying as he lies there. [18] Lift the boy up and take him by the hand, for I will make him into a great nation." [19] Then God opened her eyes and she saw a well of water. So, she went and filled the skin with water and gave the boy a drink" (Genesis 21:17-19 NIV).

The appearance of the well from which Hagar and the boy drank from was not a creative miracle, otherwise, the Bible would have said so. The well was always there, but Hagar could not see it, because she was blinded to it. In the same vein, you could be in a place where there are loads of opportunities, and yet not see them. You could be in a place where there is an abundance of resources, and still be in need. You could be amid a crowd and still feel lonely, until you locate someone you can connect with. You need God to open your eyes so you can see what is available for you, in the place where you are planted. I had an experience that I cannot forget because the Lord used it to share with me the need for God to open someone's eyes, for him to see the blessings of God around him.

I recall that evening when I discovered the beautiful park at the back of our home in Sheffield. We had lived in the house for over ten years, but I did not know such a place existed until that beautiful day when I stumbled into it while on my usual walk. Right behind where we live is this beautiful place, full of all kinds of trees, and fruits, and fantastic pathways. Sheffield is built on seven hills, and the park was at the edge of one of the hills, having a great vantage point, on which you could have beautiful view of Sheffield city centre, and much of other parts of the city. It was an exhilarating scene, and I was very excited about the discovery, so I sat on a bench made of rusted wood that I saw in the area, enjoying the cool evening breeze and praying over Sheffield. Then I heard the Lord speak to me. He spoke to me in a way and manner of which He had spoken only few times before, but it was clear and unmistakable. He said to me, "This city is blessed. There is so much in the land that you can have and enjoy. I led you to this place because I wanted you to know that it is possible to live in a place that is filled with many good things and still be blind to them until I open your eyes. I can open your eyes to see what I have put in the city."

You need God to open your eyes so you can see the doors that are opened to you and the opportunities that are presenting themselves to you. You must ask God to open your eyes in order to recognize your destiny helpers. You need God to open your eyes so you can see your harvests that are ripe and ready to be plucked.

> "Say not ye, there are yet four months, and then cometh harvest? behold, I say unto you, Lift up your eyes, and look on the fields; for they are white already to harvest" (John 4:35 KJV).

You will miss a lot and end up going in circles, not achieving what you need to if you are blind and cannot see what is there and available to you. One of the devil's powerful arsenals against people achieving success is blindness. He likes to keep people blind to what is out there and available to them, so they do not enjoy living and blame God for not caring for them and failing to answer their prayers.

> "In whom the god of this world hath blinded the minds of them which believe not, lest the light of the glorious gospel of Christ, who is the image of God, should shine unto them" (2 Corinthians 4:4 KJV).

If you are blind, an opportunity that has the potential to transform your life and situation will appear to you as a waste of your time. You will view a brilliant and revolutionary idea as a bad idea and a foolish thing to do. If you are blind and cannot see clearly, your destiny helpers—people that the Lord led to you because they are relevant to your destiny—will seem to you as your enemies of progress, and you would be praying them away. And you may be in a place that is so blessed for your sake and is having in abundance what you need, but it is not going to reflect on you, they will not benefit you. People will move into town and settle long after you did, and they will see what you couldn't see, and they will seize the opportunities they see, and they will go on to achieve many good things for themselves, leaving you wondering how you missed the opportunities they saw; however, they have been right there all along.

You must make Ephesians 1:17-18 your constant prayer guide. Paul prayed it constantly for the Ephesian church thus:

"That the God of our Lord Jesus Christ, the Father of glory, may give unto you the spirit of wisdom and revelation in the knowledge of him: [18] The eyes of your understanding being enlightened; that ye may know what the hope of his calling is, and what the riches of the glory of his inheritance in the saints" (Ephesians 1:17-18 KJV).

Pray constantly that the eyes of your understanding be enlightened, that you may know what the hope of his calling is and what the riches of the glory of his inheritance are in you. Never forget, there is everything you need in the place God has planted you.

OPEN DOOR SOMETIMES COME IN FORM OF AN OPPORTUNITY

I've used the words "open doors" and "opportunities" interchangeably throughout this chapter because they can mean the same thing. Opportunities frequently lead to open doors. Always be on the lookout for an opportunity, especially an opportunity for the six things that I enumerated at the beginning of this chapter. Make it one of your core values to never despise opportunities, even when they appear small or not attractive, because you never can tell where they will lead to. Never ignore an opportunity for you to show some kindness to someone, you may never know, the opportunity could be a chance for you to encounter an Angel. There are angels moving about in human form, and many people have unknowingly, bypassed them, ignoring the urge to give them a hand of help, thinking they were dealing with a fellow human being.

"Keep on loving one another as brothers and sisters. [2] Do not forget to show hospitality to strangers, for by so doing some people have shown hospitality to angels without knowing it." (Hebrews 13:1-2 NIV).

The hospitality some people gave to angels as stated in the scripture above literally means so. However, you can never tell, the person you show kindness to today, may be the human angel you are going to need to get to somewhere important in the future. Help people whenever the opportunity presents itself, especially if you have the means to make a difference. Do not let any opportunity to show some kindness escape you. Being helpful to strangers in need–those who cannot pay you back in return–is a wonderful opportunity.

An opportunity to serve is also another good chance you have. Be not wary of serving whenever there is a such opportunity and serve well and from your heart. The place of service is a powerful place to get blessed. Another important value to instil is that you should never live your life solely for yourself or for material benefits. You must learn to volunteer to work in your church, your community, and in some charity organisations and not asking for pay. Always grab the opportunity to volunteer to give extra hours at your workplace, giving your time to do what you notice is left undone without demanding extra pay. You will be setting yourself up for success, having these as a life principle. You can never get it wrong committing to a life of voluntary service.

As I close this chapter, I encourage you to start maximizing your time today. Pay attention to the open doors or opportunities God is giving you each new day and seek an effective way to utilize them. Remember that you will be forfeiting so much if you cannot recognize open doors or are not conscious of time and timing. Here are two tragic ways you can misuse your time (I). Thinking you have all the time (II). Procrastinating and moving the things you are to do today to tomorrow.

Chapter 8

WATCH OUT FOR THE ENEMIES OF YOUR PROGRESS

"For a great door and effectual is opened unto me, and there are many adversaries." (1 Corinthians 16:9 KJV).

When a great door opens for you, a pathway for you to achieve progress will show forth, and God will release the accompanying grace to enable you to thrive on the pathway. You will then begin to have remarkable success as you walk it, and your life will change for the better. God opens doors primarily to assist you in accomplishing something new and making an impact in your spheres of influence. However, you will also notice that adversaries against your success will start to emerge. It is through the emergence of your newfound grace, your breakthrough, and your success that you will see that not everyone who is around you is happy to see you succeed. Many adversaries will rise and will try to hinder you. They will emerge from unusual places, and some of the people who will become adversaries are those you least expect.

There are many people around you who are happy for you to stay as you are, and your sudden rise will infuriate them. You expect that they will celebrate your new success. Unfortunately, they wish you a different outcome. It is critical that you become aware of these adversaries and are well-prepared to deal with them. Your adversaries who may have any advantage over you, and succeed in derailing you, would be those who you are ignorant of, or those you are aware of but are ignoring, and doing nothing about your safety. Also, those who may have advantage over you and succeed in harming you, will be the ones whose scheming and ploys you are ignorant of. You must realise that you are always at a disadvantage when you are ignorant of Satan's devices. Bible says, "Lest Satan should get an advantage of us: for we are not ignorant of his devices" (2 Corinthians 2:11 KJV). Do not be naïve, do not take anything for granted, ask the Lord to unveil to you all the activities ongoing around you, and for Him to help you be a step ahead.

SATAN IS THE ENEMY

You must seek to know who your adversaries are, and you must seek to understand their tools and schemes. More importantly, as a believer, you must always have it in the back of your mind that, though we may contend with human beings, our main adversary is Satan himself and not people.

> "Be sober, be vigilant; because your adversary the devil, as a roaring lion, walketh about, seeking whom he may devour" (1 Peter 5:8 KJV).

Satan seeks to stand on your way, anytime he sees that God is doing something new in your life. He always wants to counter God and reverse whatever God does; because he still covets God's position, and to even rise above God. Satan the devil hates to see you successful and fulfilled, because that is what God wants for you. Satan is always opposite to God; while God wants you to have life, and to have it more abundantly, Satan seeks to steal from you, kill and destroy what is yours (John 10:10). No matter the case, you must always remember that Satan has no capacity to overpower God. He cannot close the door that God opens. In his effort to stand in your way and resist your advancement, he will try to distract you, take your attention away from the direction you should go, or make you blind so you cannot see what God is doing. He will also attack you spiritually; Satan and his evil spirits cannot directly operate physically.

He will try to kill your spiritual fire by making you trivialize sinful behaviors during the spiritual attack. He will seek to drain your anointing by making you disobedient to God. He will seek to interfere with your spiritual devotion and relationship with the Lord by luring you to pursue physical and material things more than you seek God. He knows that you can only be spiritual to the extent that you are also vibrant in your pursuit of God. If Satan is successful in distracting you from spiritual matters and causing you to pray less, he will limit your progress and minimize your success.

SATAN'S USE OF HUMAN BEING TO ACHIEVE HIS PURPOSE

Satan does not only fight people spiritually. He also makes use of human beings to achieve his purposes. He will stir up people against you in an effort to stop you from actualizing God's promises for you. Therefore, you are going to encounter human enemies—people who will hate you for no reason, people who will stand to oppose you and seek to make your life uncomfortable for no reason. Some of the people Satan will try to use against you will be your friends and even family members, and they will turn against you. You must not be surprised if you witness all these things happening to you because Jesus said:

> "If the world hate you, ye know that it hated me before it hated you. [19] If ye were of the world, the world would love his own: but because ye are not of the world, but I have chosen you out of the world, therefore the world hateth you" (John 15:18-19 KJV).

You must always remember that not everybody will always like you. People will hate you for your guts, for your vision, for your standing with Jesus, for your success, and for your values. Whatever the case, you must understand and always remember that, as a believer, you are to see only the devil as your enemy and see him as the one behind every human adversary.

107

YOUR WARFARE IS AGAINST SATAN AND NOT PEOPLE

You must understand that just because God said something about you, it does not mean that your enemy Satan will go to sleep regarding it. He will unleash all forces at his disposal to stop God's word concerning you from happening. So, you must go to war with him. You must engage in warfare with all forces, contend with them, and keep what is given to you by God. Critically, however, you must have the understanding that you are to engage in your warfare only against the devil and not with people.

> "For we wrestle not against flesh and blood, but against principalities, against powers, against the rulers of the darkness of this world, against spiritual wickedness in high places" (Ephesians 6:12 KJV).

The devil does not want you to know who your real enemies are; fighting with people will never win you the battle. The devil does not also want you to discover the tools he has fashioned against you, pray that God will show them to you. Though, sometimes, you will have to contend with people, the devil will stir them up to fight you, however, you must love all people, have an open mind, and maintain a positive attitude towards all, reaching out to relate with all people, in love and care. Not dealing with people out of fear, not being suspicious of everyone's motives, and wondering if they are there to harm you. The fact that the devil will make use of people to try to harm you, does not mean all the people around you, are there to harm you. Not having a positive attitude towards everyone and living in suspicion of everyone is a torturous way to live. You will not have, and enjoy a quality life, and a healthy relationship, if there is no trust in your relationships with people.

Trust is one of the pillars of a healthy relationship. Relationships become weak and torturous when trust is lacking. You must live your life free of fear, being confident and bold, having a sense of security, and being fully aware that you are under God's protection. I am not suggesting that you be naive about the realities of life and people's tendency to be susceptible to being used by Satan, the enemy. Do not forget that satanic weapons will only be successful against you when you are naive and ignorant of his works (2 Corinthians 2:11 KJV). It is therefore expedient to be aware of the forces you are contending with, at every level, and what their weapons of war against you are.

As much as you love people and relate to them with an open mind, you must still be aware that not everyone around you is really interested in your welfare and is happy to see you succeed. Every believer can take solace in the fact that those who support them will always outnumber those who oppose them.

> "And he answered, Fear not: for they that be with us are more
> than they that be with them" (2 Kings 2:16 KJV).

THE HUMAN ADVERSARIES

As David was nearing his time of death, he counselled Solomon, his son and successor to his throne. And he exposes to Solomon the kinds of people who are near the throne, with whom Solomon will have to contend. David revealed to Solomon how some specific individuals in the kingdom have behaved toward the throne, and he instructed Solomon to deal with them in his wisdom (1 Kings 2:1-9). In the same vein, if you are a praying person and you are obedient to God, God will reveal to you the kinds of people you are being surrounded with, or you are going to encounter, so that you will know how to behave in wisdom towards them. He will show you your enemies and the things they are doing to try to stop you or harm you. These people manifest in different forms and shades.

★ Frenemy Adversary

> "Frenemy" is an oxymoron. It refers to someone who presents
> himself as both a friend and an enemy. A frenemy is someone
> who combines the characteristics of a friend and an enemy.

You must be aware that your sudden rise to prominence and success will attract enemies—those who do not like you but are drawn to you because of what they can gain from you. They are never wholeheartedly with you. Commitment only makes sense to them for as long as the conditions are right. You need God to open your eyes to know the kind of people you have in your life.

The frenemy is **JUDAS' SPIRIT**

He is someone who is part of your life and your friend, but he competes with you, and whenever it comes to personal gain, he will sell you out, and kiss you goodbye, without a second thought.

> "Then one of the Twelve, the one called Judas Iscariot went to the chief priests [15] and asked, "What are you willing to give me if I deliver him over to you?" So, they counted out for him thirty pieces of silver. [16] From then on Judas watched for an opportunity to hand him over (Matthew 26:14-16 NIV).

Selfishness, greed, and envy are the motivating forces behind Judas' self-seeking spirit. Envy is the most lethal. They become enraged when good things happen to you. They wish the good thing had happened to them instead. Mark, the one who gave us the gospel of Mark, shares that one of the reasons why Judas betrayed Jesus was his indignation at the kind gesture of a certain woman toward Jesus. She came to Jesus with an alabaster box of ointment, very precious and expensive ointment, and broke it and poured all the contents on Jesus. It angered Judas. He preferred that it was sold instead, so he could have the opportunity to steal from the prosit of it. In indignation, he left them and went to the chief priests to betray Jesus.

> "And being in Bethany in the house of Simon the leper, as he sat at meat, there came a woman having an alabaster box of ointment of spikenard very precious; and she brake the box, and poured it on his head. [4] And there were some that had indignation within themselves, and said, Why was this waste

of the ointment made? [5] For it might have been sold for more than three hundred pence, and have been given to the poor. And they murmured against her. [6] And Jesus said, Let her alone; why trouble ye her? she hath wrought a good work on me. [7] For ye have the poor with you always, and whensoever ye will ye may do them good: but me ye have not always. [8] She hath done what she could: she is come aforehand to anoint my body to the burying. [9] Verily I say unto you, Wheresoever this gospel shall be preached throughout the whole world, this also that she hath done shall be spoken of for a memorial of her. [10] And Judas Iscariot, one of the twelve, went unto the chief priests, to betray him unto them" (Mark 14:3-10 KJV).

The Judas spirit was what Jacob's uncle, Laban, had. He was like family to him, and he was even married to Laban's two daughters, but he tried to defraud Jacob and keep him as a perpetual servant, but God was with Jacob, and he used Laban's schemes to make Jacob extremely wealthy. This is how Jacob puts it.

"It was like this for the twenty years I was in your household. I worked for you fourteen years for your two daughters and six years for your flocks, and you changed my wages ten times. [42] If the God of my father, the God of Abraham, and the Fear of Isaac, had not been with me, you would surely have sent me away empty-handed. But God has seen my hardship and the toil of my hands, and last night he rebuked you" (Genesis 31:41-42 NIV).

The same spirit worked in Joseph's brothers as well, and they sold him away out of envy, but God turned his fortune around, and by the time they saw him next, he had risen to royalty. Joseph said to his brothers:

"You intended to harm me, but God intended it for good to accomplish what is now being done, the saving of many lives" (Genesis 50:20 NIV).

People with Judas' spirit always base their relationships on personal gains. It will be all about what they can get from it. And when they get the opportunity, they will steal from you—steal your ideas, steal your connections, betray your trust, and sell you out without a second thought. They are happy to make profits at your expense. Judas' spirit will walk away very easily at the opening of a better alternative and leave you stranded at the time you needed them the most.

You can recognize the spirit of Judas easily because it will always make excuses and not be there for you when you need them the most, or when someone needs to pay a price to make something happen. They will hardly make sacrifices for you and whenever they do so, it is with ulterior motive. You will notice that the Judas spirit is often missed when it is a trying season, they will be at the other side of you, just as Judas was on the other side with the soldiers, and not with Jesus. It is a pain to have a Judas's spirit as a friend or partner, however, sometimes, their presence is necessary for you to reach your destiny. Satan will use them to sell you out, he will mean it for evil, however, their betrayal will open you up to a brand-new world.

It is critical that you ask God to help you determine if you have a foe closing in on you. It will help you behave wisely in how you go about your relationship with them. Jesus knew who Judas was even before he chose him to be one of the twelve disciples. Jesus knew that Judas was a thief and that he would bring him pain, but He still let him into his circle because he also knew that the pain Judas will bring, will pave the way for Redemption.

> "Jesus answered them, Have not I chosen you twelve, and one of you is a devil? [71] He spake of Judas Iscariot the son of Simon: for he it was that should betray him, being one of the twelve" (John 6:70-71 KJV).

★ The upfront adversary

I call them upfront adversaries because, as the name suggests, these adversaries are people who are confident enough to let you know, or tell you, from the onset and to your face, where their position with you is. They are not afraid of you or hypocritical about you, and they let you know outright that they do not like you and that they are against you, and they are not apologetic about it.

It is easier to deal with upfront adversaries because there is nothing secretive about their feelings toward you. They do not like you, and they want you to know it. These are the people who are not happy about anything good that happens to you. They show it, and they fight to upturn it.

The upfront adversaries are always plotting against you. They are always looking for any chance to do you harm, and they know you are aware of it, and they do not care. They like to portray you as a bad person, and they criticize you no matter what good you do. These people resist every move you make to make things right with them because they do not want any peace between you.

The upfront adversaries are also the people who like to get you in trouble at your work place, so they can get you fired. They hate to be in the same room with you. If they discover that you both have common friends, they cut off from the other person, as they cannot have anything in common with you. They believe that their friends should be enemies of their enemies, and their friends must be friends of their friends.

The upfront adversary is **THE SAULS SPIRIT**

> "And Saul was very wroth, and the saying displeased him; and he said, They have ascribed unto David ten thousands, and to me they have ascribed but thousands: and what can he have more but the kingdom? [9] And Saul eyed David from that day and forward. [10] And it came to pass on the morrow, that

113

the evil spirit from God came upon Saul, and he prophesied in the midst of the house: and David played with his hand, as at other times: and there was a javelin in Saul's hand. [11] And Saul cast the javelin; for he said, I will smite David even to the wall with it. And David avoided out of his presence twice." (1 Samuel 18:8-11 KJV)

Saul did not keep his hatred for David or his desire to kill him a secret. Saul planned to kill him and threw a javelin at him in front of everyone in the king's palace. He also mobilized a battalion of his army and went hunting for David to destroy him. All because David killed Goliath, and the people sang his praises. The spirit that drives the opponent in the foreground is the spirit of hate and envy. You do not have to do anything wrong to the people who carry Saul's spirit to make them hate you, just being on the right side of history, and succeeding suffices it. You cannot, not succeed, because of these types of people in your circle. You must not hold back from achieving your dreams because you are concerned that, some people who are around you, may be infuriated by your success.

You cannot submit yourself to failure because it will make some people happy. That will be insane. You cannot live in fear of being successful or be afraid to publicly declare the goodness of God in your life. If you know who your adversaries are, the best way to deal with them is to stay away from them. Stay away from people who have expressed their desire to harm you and have stated that they will do so if given the opportunity. Ensure that you do not hate them back, love them from your heart. However, stay far away from them, as much as possible, praying for them that they will encounter God and be saved.

Furthermore, you must constantly engage the spirit, in these people, in a constant warfare, bringing them under subjection. You must be clear on the fact that these set of people are not born again, and that is why they hate you. And it really does not matter whether they say they are born again or not, and whether they go to church or not. John the apostle told us that anyone who hates does not know God.

"He that loveth his brother abideth in the light, and there is none occasion of stumbling in him. [11] But he that hateth his brother is in darkness, and walketh in darkness, and knoweth not whither he goeth, because that darkness hath blinded his eyes". (1 John 2:10-11 KJV)

"If a man say, I love God, and hateth his brother, he is a liar: for he, that loveth not his brother whom he hath seen, how can he love God whom he hath not seen." (1 John 4:20 KJV).

Loving the people who hate you is by itself a powerful defence against the weapon of hate. Hating the people who hate you back, will make you weak and vulnerable. However, if you are good to them, you will, through your good, conquer the evil in them. That is what the Bible says - "Don't let evil conquer you, but conquer evil by doing good." (Romans 12:21 NLT). Furthermore, Jesus says, "...I say unto you, Love your enemies, bless them that curse you, do good to them that hate you, and pray for them which despitefully use you, and persecute you." (Matthew 5:44 KJV). If you do good to them that hate you, whenever you get the chance to, they are not going to be able to prevail against you, no matter what scheme they deploy. That was why the Holy Spirit smote David's conscience when he cut Saul's garment in the cave, even though Saul was the aggressor (1 Samuel 24: 1-7). Paying them back hate for hate, evil for evil, and wishing and praying them to die, is going to be counterproductive. We are instructed in the scriptures thus:

"Never pay back evil with more evil. Do things in such a way that everyone can see you are honorable. [18] Do all that you can to live in peace with everyone. [19] Dear friends, never take revenge. Leave that to the righteous anger of God. For the Scriptures say, "I will take revenge; I will pay them back," says the LORD. [20] Instead, "If your enemies are hungry, feed them. If they are thirsty, give them something to drink. In doing this, you will heap burning coals of shame on their heads." [21] Don't let evil conquer you, but conquer evil by doing good." (Romans 12:17-21 NLT).

★ The Covert adversary

The covert adversaries are people who show outwardly that they like you, and they also give the impression that they are always on your side. However, behind your back, they work against you. There are two types of covert adversaries: (I). The first types are the people with whom you are familiar with, you think they are on your side, and that they are supportive of you, but they are not, and you are not aware of that. (II) The second types of people are the people you have no clue exist, but they are around you, watching you like a wild cat, and waiting for a chance to pounce on you. Covert enemies are always watching you and waiting for a chance to hurt you, even if you don't know they're there.

The word "covert" means that these adversaries work underground, they are secret enemies, they could be in your neighbourhood, they could be in your church, they could be in your school or at your workplace, and are busy doing things to undermine your effort, and to hurt you, but you have no knowledge of it. You may sometimes notice that certain things are going wrong for you, and you will be wondering why that is happening, but unknown to you, these covert adversaries are at work causing you harm. I pray that God will expose all the people who are fighting against you in secret, in Jesus' name. Amen!

Covert adversaries do not want you to know they exist. Those that you have not met do everything to avoid meeting you face to face; they enjoy being anonymous; their strength is in their secrecy. Since the strength of the covert adversary is in secrecy, it often collapses when they are uncovered. They fight you secretly because even though they do not like you, they cannot stand up against you face to face. The convert adversary could be your neighbour, who do not want you in the neighbourhood, he thinks you do not fit the pedigree of those who can live there. He could be a colleague at your workplace who is not happy that you were employed in the company. He wanted the role you got, he sees you as an intruder, and behind the scenes he is doing stuff to undermine your competence, and make you look bad. Covert adversary may also be someone you offended in the past, and you think you made it up with him, and have moved on, but he did not, he is still hurting, and keeping malice, and is looking for a chance to hurt you back.

To avoid unnecessary animosity, it is critical that whenever there is a disagreement between you and someone, you always deal with it forcefully and reach a healthy conclusion. Covert adversaries could also be people who wrongly perceive that you are against them. Possibly, because of an incident that happened in the past, which you treated as insignificant, but they did not see it so, and as a result, have vowed to pay you back, and you have no clues about it.

I have seen all kinds of cases relating to this where people have developed resentments against someone, and the person is not even aware of it. I know a case, where two friends went to the same interview for a job, and one of them got the job. Unknown to the one who got the job, the other friend felt betrayed. He had expected that the friend who got the job would have withdrawn and not go for the interview because he already had a job, while the other one did not. I also know of another case, where two friends, ladies, fell in love with the same guy secretly, he was a friend to both of them, none of them shared their feelings with the other, and both of them were hoping he will propose, and when he proposed to one of them, the other pretended she was happy for her, but it was not genuine, and have since then, seen the friend as someone who stole her lover, and took away her source of happiness, and she hates her secretly and is wishing her evil.

Covert adversaries like to come across as being so nice and helpful that you will never think that there are issues between you and them. Though you may never come into contact with them and have no direct dealings with them, they are always closing in on you and working against you. And except the Lord exposes them and turns their schemes into nothing, they will do terrible harm.

The covert adversary is **THE ABSALOMS SPIRIT**

"And Absalom rose up early, and stood beside the way of the gate: and it was so, that when any man that had a controversy came to the king for judgment, then Absalom called unto him, and said, Of what city art thou? And he said, Thy servant is of one of the tribes of Israel. [3] And Absalom said unto him, See, thy matters are good and right; but there is no man deputed of the king to hear thee. [4] Absalom said moreover, Oh that I were made judge in the land, that every man which hath any suit or cause might come unto me, and I would do him justice! [5] And it was so, that when any man came nigh to him to do him obeisance, he put forth his hand, and took him, and kissed him. [6] And on this manner did Absalom to all Israel that came to the king for judgment: so, Absalom stole the hearts of the men of Israel." (2 Samuel 15:2-6 KJV)

Absalom was David's son he lived in the palace, feeding off David's wealth, and enjoying all the privileges of the king's son, however, he covets after his father's throne, and he secretly planned the overthrowing of his father. Unknown to David, Absalom, his son, had an eye on his throne, and he stood by the palace gate each morning and intercepted the people as they came to see the king. Absalom schemed his way into the people's hearts, by presenting himself as a better king than David, suggesting to the people that he would give a better judgement for them, if he were the king. Through scheming, and under David's radar, Absalom won the people's allegiance, then, he mobilised them to overthrow David. The spirit behind the covert adversary is the spirit of pride, greed, unforgiveness, and bitterness. These were the negative forces found in Absalom, and they contributed to ruining him. His pride, due to his handsomeness, made him think he could be a better kind than his father. Also, he had kept an unsettled score with his father.

Absalom's bitterness against David stemmed from the humiliation his sister Tamara went through when their half-brother Amnon raped her and dumped her, and David did nothing about it. Tamar was a virgin and a beautiful woman. Another of David's sons, Amnon, their half-brother, fell in love with Tamar, then lured her, and raped her and then rejected her in disgrace. For two years Absalom her brother, from the same mother, kept silent, sheltering Tamar in his home. He had expected that their father, David, the King, would punish Amnon for his wickedness toward Tamar, but when David did nothing, Absalom vengefully plotted and killed Amnon. Absalom fled after the assassination. However, after a period, David missed Absalom deeply, and he allowed him to come back to Jerusalem. But, from that point forward, Absalom began to undermine King David, usurping his authority and speaking to the people in order to turn their hearts against David.

You should be wary of anyone close to you who has not forgiven you from the bottom of his heart for any wrong you have done to them. You can tell they did not completely forgive you because you can see that, though they smile at you, their attitude toward you has changed. They no longer visit as before, they no longer pick up your calls, and they take their time before they return your text messages, or your missed calls. Also, you will notice that they like to remind you of how you hurt them in the past. You will also notice that sometimes they join other people in opposing your position, even though they claim that it is in your interest. They speak against you behind your back, and you sometimes get to hear the things they say. You must be wary of anyone in your circle who is doing things to undermine you, present themselves as better, and seek to take people's attention and interest away from you. That is Absalom's spirit in operation.

★ The make-believe/chameleon adversary

The difference between the chameleon and the covert adversary is that the chameleon adversary is in your life, as part of your team, and there is some sort of bond that exists between you. The chameleon always blends in, and is actively involved with you, however, he is with you only to serve his own interests. The chameleon wants you to believe that your domain is his habitat, but it is not his reality. It is a fallacy, he is only enduring it, being there. On the inside, he feels very differently about you than he is letting on. He is comfortable in your domain, only for as long as he is getting what he wants. With the lips the chameleon will praise you, but on the inside of him, he is cursing you. He will smile at you but on the inside of him, he is wishing you bad. He is empathising with you when you are in difficulty but in his heart, he is celebrating your misfortune. He shows he is interested in your success, but inside him, he is envious of you and is covetousness of your place. When you achieve success, he rejoices with you outwardly, but inside, he wishes you had failed. If he gets the chance, he will bring you down and replace you.

The chameleon talks well of you before you, but behind you, they defame your character. They want everyone to see you as a bad person. They present themselves as your friends and family, but they are enemies, wolves in sheep's clothing. The chameleon is the deadliest kind of adversary. The worst enemy is the one within, not the one out there. He is someone you have received as being a part of you, trust and treat as good person. He is someone you believe you are having a good relationship with; you open and share your personal life with, but unknown to you, they are seeking your downfall. Chameleons are only a make-believe friend, putting up an appearance of friendship but they are not, it is a fallacy.

The chameleon will pose as being helpful, counselling you. However, they are misleading, it is the wrong counsel. You must be careful with the friend who is suggesting you quit school, resign from your job, quit your marriage, leave your church, unfriend people etc. Your failure, downfalls, lack of progression, is intoxicating to them. The chameleon adversary is someone who will withhold vital information from you, knowing that it will help you achieve greater success. They like to know your weaknesses, so they will use them against you when they get the chance. They may even arm your enemies with information about you to harm you. They steal your ideas and use them before you get to do it, and when you complain, they turn it against you, making you feel like an enemy of progress.

You must be careful about who you bring into your inner chambers. Know them very well first, and prayerfully, before you disclose your personal life to them. Never ignore any irritation you receive in your spirit, in your dealings with people, no matter the level of trust you have for them. Be careful about who knows how much you are worth. A good example to learn from that relates to the make-believe adversary is the story of Hezekiah, the king of Judah, who, out of naivety, showed his wealth and the glory of his kingdom to an enemy who presented himself as a friend, and as a result, he lost everything to him; his kingdom, consequently, was effectively invaded.

> "At that time Merodach-baladan, the son of Baladan, king of Babylon, sent letters and a present to Hezekiah: for he had heard that he had been sick, and was recovered. [2] And Hezekiah was glad of them, and shewed them the house of his precious things, the silver, and the gold, and the spices, and the precious ointment, and all the house of his armour, and all that was found in his treasures: there was nothing in his house, nor in all his dominion, that Hezekiah shewed them not. [3] Then came Isaiah the prophet unto king Hezekiah, and said unto him, what said these men? and from whence came they unto thee? And Hezekiah said, they are come from a far country unto me, even from Babylon. [4] Then said he, what have they seen in thine house? And Hezekiah answered, all that is in mine house have they seen: there is nothing among my treasures that I have not shewed them. [5] Then said Isaiah to Hezekiah, Hear the word of the Lord of hosts: [6] Behold, the days come, that all that is in thine house, and that which thy fathers have laid up in store until this day, shall be carried to Babylon: nothing shall be left, saith the Lord. [7] And of thy sons that shall issue from thee, which thou shalt beget, shall they take away; and they shall be eunuchs in the palace of the king of Babylon. [8] Then said Hezekiah to Isaiah, Good is the word of the Lord which thou hast spoken. He said moreover, for there shall be peace and truth in my days" (Isaiah 39:1-8 KJV).

The issue with King Hezekiah was that he was naive and overly trusting of people with whom he had little or no dealings. Despite the fact that the visitors from Babylon had not been vetted and that they were all strangers to him, he opened the entire treasure house to them, exposing the glory of his kingdom to the people who coveted it and would one day return to take them away by force. You must be careful about who sees into your storehouse. You must be careful about who gets to hear your vision and brilliant ideas before you are ready to act on them. You must be careful about who you pour out your heart to because you may unknowingly be arming someone who is an adversary. You must be cautious about who you sit with and reveal the deepest secrets of your heart to; it is critical that not everyone who comes close knows and sees everything about you.

The chameleon/make-believe adversary is **THE CAINS SPIRIT**

> "And Cain talked with Abel his brother: and it came to pass, when they were in the field, that Cain rose up against Abel his brother, and slew him." (Genesis 4:8 KJV).

Abel trusted Cain, he was his biological brother, and he loved him. And when Cain asked for them to go on a walk in the field, Abel obliged him. Abel thought that he was safe in the company of his own brother Cain, but unfortunately for Abel, Cain had become envious of him and begrudged him because of the favour he had found before God. While they were in the field, unsuspectedly, Cain cowardly slew his brother Abel out of envy.

The Cain spirit is the spirit of envy, rivalry, unhealthy competition, and the feeling of superiority and pride. You should be wary of friends who like to feel superior to you, friends who compete with you, and friends who want what you have. You should be cautious of friends who do not appear happy when good things happen to you, and friends who like to keep information from you so that you do not know as much as them and do not achieve as much success as them.

The people who envy you and covet your position are going to stand in your way when they get the chance, or even do harmful things to you, to make you fail. You must be careful how you share your dreams and ideas, especially with people who envy you. They will steal it and go to implement it before you do. And by the time you get around to doing it, it will appear as though you stole the ideas from them. They will also take your secrets and sell you out, exposing your nakedness before the people who will use such information to hurt you.

★ Ignorant tools adversary

People who can become your ignorant tools adversaries are typically those who genuinely love, care about, and will always protect you. The devil knows the people in your circle, and he knows where each one's heart is toward you. Sometimes Satan does not make use of the people who are obvious to you as being against you. Instead, he uses the people you know love and care about you. Satan likes to pick on them and use them against you because he knows that you trust them and will pay attention to whatever they say.

The ignorant tools of our adversaries operate in ignorance and are usually not aware that they are being used as tools by Satan. These people genuinely care about you, they will not knowingly, and intentionally do anything that will harm you, and Satan knows that, and that is why he selected them. People that love you and are being influenced by Satan to work against you innocently think that they are acting in your interests, and completely oblivious of Satan's influence over them. When they resist you, they think that they are serving your interest. This was the kind of spirit that was in operation in Peter when he rebuked Jesus and advised him against the laying down of His life and dying on the Cross.

> "From that time forth began Jesus to shew unto his disciples, how that he must go unto Jerusalem, and suffer many things of the elders and chief priests and scribes, and be killed, and be raised again the third day. [22] Then Peter took him, and began to rebuke him, saying, be it far from thee, Lord: this shall not be unto thee. [23] But he turned, and said unto Peter, get thee behind me, Satan: thou art an offence unto me: for

thou savourest not the things that be of God, but those that be of men" (Matthew 16:21-23 KJV).

Peter was genuine, he had a deep affinity for Jesus. When Peter spoke out against Jesus's death on the cross, he spoke out of his concern and care for Jesus. However, irrespective of the genuineness of his love for Jesus and the sincerity of his heart, his rebuke of Jesus was under the influence of Satan. Satan was in Peter, attempting to obstruct the work of redemption for which Jesus came to the world. It is critical for you to have convictions about the things you believe. It is critical for you to understand and be established in what you stand for. You cannot hang your destiny on what someone thinks, or what someone says about you, or what you hold dear to your heart. Because there are many people, who can be influenced by Satan to deceive you into going off course.

There are many people who have been deceived in our churches, and even ruined, by men and women of God, whom they trusted, a looked up to, and held in honour as anointed by God, because they absorbed everything, they said without questioning their source. If God says to test every spirit, it follows that another spirit can be in operation, even in the believers' gathering. It is possible that some prophecies given, may proceed from lying spirits, to mislead, and not from God.

> "Do not treat prophecies with contempt [21] but test them all; hold on to what is good, [22] reject every kind of evil" (1 Thessalonians 5:20-22 NIV)

You must know that it is possible for any man to speak in error and out of his own wishes, not under the inspiration of the Holy Spirit, even if he is a man of God. Only God is perfect and does everything right, and no human being is. You must know that you are going to fall into error if you simply take anything anyone says, without first testing the source of what is said, using the word of God as a yardstick. Someone would ask, is it possible for a man of God to speak in error? Of course, it is possible. There was a man of God in the Scriptures, who once spoke in error as well.

"After David was settled in his palace, he said to Nathan the prophet, "Here I am, living in a house of cedar, while the ark of the covenant of the Lord is under a tent." [2] Nathan replied to David, "Whatever you have in mind, do it, for God is with you." [3] But that night the word of God came to Nathan, saying: [4] "Go and tell my servant David, 'This is what the Lord says: You are not the one to build me a house to dwell in" (1 Chronicles 17:1-4 NIV)

The scripture above shows us how prophet Nathan, in his excitement, was hasty in saying to David the king that God is with him, and that God has approved for David to build God's temple. However, he spoke too quickly, and he did not hear from God when he responded to David, approving him to go ahead and build for God. Thank God Nathan was humble enough, and he corrected himself when God instructed him to withdraw the message he gave to David. How many men and women of God in our churches have come back to reverse the wrong messages they preached, or the prophecies they gave to people in error? You must increase your knowledge of the Bible, train yourself to discern prophecy, and learn to receive direct messages from God.

It is important that everyone be careful about the role he plays in people's lives, particularly the people they have some influence over. People such as their spouses, their children, their students, the members of their congregation etc. You must avoid playing God in their lives. Your advice should always be not only good advice but also godly advice. You must ensure that your counsel always lines up with God's word and is given from the integrity of your heart. See to it that your motive is always right, not serving your selfish interests, but the interests of the people you seek to help. You have a duty to ensure that Satan does not use you to take advantage of anyone or remove them from what is God's will for them. Nobody's life should be ruined because of the role you played in it.

Furthermore, you must watch out for pride and not insist that someone listen to what you say because you think your opinion is superior to theirs. You must watch out for your controlling attitude and drop it. It is a controlling attitude to insist that people must do things your way. You must watch out for the myopic mindset. The general believe that something should be done in a particular way, for it to be acceptable to God. God is a dynamic God. His standard is consistent. However, He does things in different methods. He can heal the blind by spitting on the floor, making clay out of it, and having someone rub it on the eye, wash it, and see. And He can also heal the blind by laying hands on them and healing them.

The ignorant tools adversary is **THE OLD PROPHETS SPIRIT**

"Now there was a certain old prophet living in Bethel, whose sons came and told him all that the man of God had done there that day. They also told their father what he had said to the king. [12] Their father asked them, "Which way did he go?" And his sons showed him which road the man of God from Judah had taken. [13] So he said to his sons, "Saddle the donkey for me." And when they had saddled the donkey for him, he mounted it [14] and rode after the man of God. He found him sitting under an oak tree and asked, "Are you the man of God who came from Judah?" "I am," he replied. [15] So the prophet said to him, "Come home with me and eat." [16] The man of God said, "I cannot turn back and go with you, nor can I eat bread or drink water with you in this place. [17] I have been told by the word of the Lord: 'You must not eat bread or drink water there or return by the way you came.'" [18] The old prophet answered, "I too am a prophet, as you are. And an angel said to me by the word of the Lord: 'Bring him back with you to your house so that he may eat bread and drink water.'" (But he was lying to him.) [19] So the man of God returned with him and ate and drank in his house. [20] While they were sitting at the table, the word of the Lord came to the old prophet who had brought him back. [21] He cried out to the man of God who had come from Judah, "This is what the Lord says: 'You have defied the word of the Lord and have not kept the command the Lord your God gave you. [22] You came back and ate bread and drank water in the place where he told you not to eat or drink. Therefore, your body will not be buried in the tomb of your ancestors.'" [23] When the man of God had finished eating and drinking, the prophet who had brought him back saddled his donkey for him. [24] As he went on his way, a lion met him on the road and killed him, and his body was left lying on the road, with both the donkey and the lion standing beside it" (1 Kings 13:11-24 NIV).

Understand that experience is great to have, but wisdom is superior to experience. Whilst experience is the product of your dealings in the affairs of life, or your knowledge acquired through your many years of doing something, wisdom is hearing from God and doing what He says. Wisdom is also knowing and following the leading of the Spirit. The young prophet abandoned what God told him to do and went for the experience of an old prophet. Respect is an honourable thing to give someone. However, you must never abandon what God told you to do out of your respect for someone, and it does not matter his genuineness or the level of his anointing.

BE WARY OF CONTROLLING SPIRIT

You are highly likely going to digress and miss out on God's promises for you the moment you come under the influence of a controlling spirit. Controlling spirits is always contrary to God's Spirit. The controlling spirit is a proud and arrogant force, and it is the old prophet's spirit. The old prophet's spirit may use age, experience, anointing, and the need to show respect to mislead.

Always remember that the old prophet's spirit is a controlling spirit, and it is the same as a witchcraft spirit. You do not have to cast a spell on people or put a curse on people, to be a witch. The fundamental thing about witchcraft, is that it seeks to influence or control people and replace God in their lives. Anyone who tries to replace God's influence over people, is practicing witchcraft (1Samuel 15: 21-22). You will be practicing witchcraft any time you try to play God in people's lives. Witchcraft expresses itself in four ways: manipulation, domination, intimidation, and control.

(I). Manipulation happens when somebody uses schemes to get people to do what he knows they will normally not do if they are let alone to use their own discretion or judgement and exert their own power of choice. The power of manipulation lies in deception.

(II). Domination is when somebody has been suppressed by another person and is not being allowed to freely express himself in the way he chooses. Domination subverts self-will and self-determination. Domination is empowered by a lack of understanding of self-worth and dignity.

(III). Control takes away someone's power of choice. It sits in the driver's seat in someone's life and makes decisions for them. Control is empowered by fear and dependence on someone. For instance, anyone who is depending on someone for his survival, may fall victim of control if he is under the fear that the means of his survival will be withdrawn, if he is not in compliant. A woman who stays with a man simply because she is afraid of the stigma that is in divorce or she is afraid of being single, or afraid she may never find somebody else can easily be a victim of control.

(IV). Intimidation happens when somebody uses threats, terror, negative reactions or emotions, or a bad attitude to get someone to do something, behave in a certain way, change his opinion or decision, and do what they want. The cure to intimidation is your boldness. It takes boldness to be able to say no when you really need to and not be afraid or feel guilty.

In this chapter, I have tried to make you realize that there are forces, both spiritually and physically, that would seek to ruin you and hinder you from achieving God's promises for you. You must not let them have an advantage over you. There is so much at stake, if you let yourself come under the influence of any negative forces, either spiritually or physically.

Remember that Satan will try to influence you in any way he can, but you must be acutely aware in these two dimensions. Maintain your spiritual alertness, and grant no man's influence over you to degree that it replaces God's influence in your life.

Conclusion

God desires to do something new in your life, He wants to change your story, and that is why He put this book in your hand. I like to hope that you read each chapter prayerfully. I released this book with a prayer, that it will carry an anointing to help the reader overcome their hindrances and move up into new heights in all spheres of their lives. I am praying that God will visit you in an incredibly unique way, and give you a new testimony, the kind that Israel had, as they departed from Egypt (Exodus 1:8-14). Israel was in Egypt for forty years under slavery. They thought God had abandoned them because Pharaoh enslaved them, and made them work tirelessly, without any reward, or a pay. However, God visited them, He showed up with mighty signs following, and they got paid of all the years of slavery in one day (Exodus 12:35-36).

I declare your supernatural breakthrough, and I decree that all limitations and blockades in your way be removed now. I declare over you a new season of harvest and the full restoration of all that Satan stole from you over many years. Now, you go forth from this moment and become more successful, stepping into the fullness of God's promises for you. May every word that resonates with you and that you take to heart throughout the pages of this book find expression in you and bring forth a great harvest in the dimensions of your dreams and desires, in the mighty name of Jesus. Amen!

Musa Bako
March 2023

Acknowledgement

All glory and praise go to the King eternal, immortal, invisible, and the only wise God for inspiring this book. I am grateful to my beautiful and adorable wife, Pastor Eunice Meque Bako, and my lovely children, Dorcas, Melissa, and Jethro, for their continuing support. I am also deeply grateful to God for the honor of being the pastor of the RCCG Victory Assembly family for the past 23 years. Thank you, VA, for partnering with me in ministry and for making pastoral work satisfying. I am proud of you all.

Other exciting books from
Musa Bako

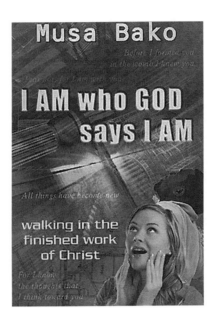

THE LOVE OF FATHER GOD

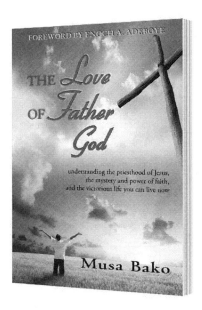

The Love of Father God unveils the heart and the never-ending love of God, the defeat and the fall of Satan, and the power and the glory of the Christian faith.

As a believer, you are a new creation in Jesus Christ—the wonder of God and the miracle of heaven. This book solves the mysteries and reveals the benefits of your role in God's kingdom.

ISBN: 978-88-96727-31-7

DESTINY IS WITHIN YOU

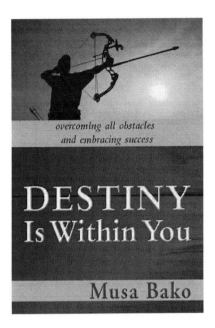

Destiny Is within You is a proven guide that enables you to achieve the goals you set for yourself in life. You will discover that God created you for a specific purpose— and you exist to accomplish your God-given destiny.

You are not a loser, a burden, or a pest. You are a unique soul with special talents and gifts, and you can enjoy a wonderfully abundant life—no matter your background, education, or current economic situation.

ISBN: 9788897896289

Everybody Needs Somebody

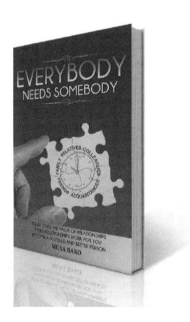

Everybody Needs Somebody was written to empower you with
tools to achieve a healthy and fruitful relationship in all spheres.
There is something great in everyone—and yes, that includes you!
Everybody has something to offer the world as unique blessings.

ISBN: 978-1-4918-7516-2

ISBN:978-1-4918-7517-9

LORD, I AM AVAILABLE; YOU CAN USE ME

Lord, I Am Available; You Can Use Me is a handbook for men and women in ministry—those who are seeking to serve God effectively and influence their generation. God will use anybody and any situation to serve His purpose. He is the Creator of all things and Lord of all the earth; He can reach out, touch, and take anything He chooses to use, but not just anyone is given a righteous assignment . . .

ISBN: 978-1-5462-9362-0

Overcoming Discouragement

MUSA BAKO

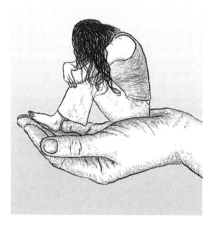

Discouragement is a spirit that feeds on human tragedies, setbacks, unfulfilled expectations, and the uncertainty of life to ruin its victims. Discouragement can attack anyone, no matter how macho they may be—no matter how brave or educated they are and no matter what achievements they have made. The attack of discouragement is one of the reasons why many people cannot move forward in life, they cannot take initiative to try something new. As a result of discouragement, many have dropped out of school, quit their job, closed their business, ended relationships, and walked away from ministry. This guide is designed to help you combat the dangers of discouragement and forge a brand-new path!

ISBN 1728354978

ISBN 978-1728354972

OVERCOMING REJECTION

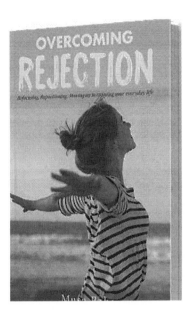

Overcoming Rejection was written with three purposes in mind. Firstly, to give readers a deeper understanding of what rejection is, the root causes, and the devastation it can cause in people who experience it, so they can avoid putting anyone in that position. Secondly, to give tools to readers who are going through rejection and empower them to deal with it appropriately, ultimately overcoming adversity. Thirdly, to provide information and tools that will help people who are supporting others struggling with rejection.

People thrive and flourish in an environment of acceptance, love, and mutual respect; therefore, no one should be made to feel unimportant. Nonetheless, rejection isn't something that anyone can completely avoid. We all will have to contend with it at some point, but Overcoming Rejection will help you to be prepared for truly anything!

ISBN:978-1685363475

ISBN: 1685363474

About the Author

Musa Bako is a mentor and executive coach. He holds a master's degree in coaching and mentoring from Sheffield Hallam University. Master in theology from Crossroads Trinity Bible College and Theology, Manchester, UK He was awarded an honorary Doctor of Theology degree from Crossroads Theological Seminary in Tallahassee, Florida, USA. He is the senior pastor of Victory Assembly (RCCG), a dynamic, growing, multicultural ministry through which God is impacting the people of Sheffield, United Kingdom, with the good news of Jesus.

Pastor Musa is also an assistant regional pastor within the RCCG. He is a sought-after speaker at conferences and has spoken at conferences in Europe, Africa, the USA, and Canada. With the grace of God on his life and thirty years in pastoral ministry, Pastor Musa teaches the Word of God with maturity, clarity, and practical insight, helping people experience the life-transforming power of God for victorious living. His ministry thrust is to equip people with the tools to succeed in life and to fulfill the reason for which they were created. His messages and writings cut across cultural boundaries. Pastor Musa is married to Pastor Eunice Meque Bako, and together they are blessed with three children.

About the Book

T he Bible is full of God's promises. The realization of these promises can make anyone enjoy supernatural living. The inspiration behind 'stepping into God's promises for you' is to resource people with tools that can assist them in seeing God's word become a reality in their lives and situations. Everything written in the Scriptures are inspired by the Holy Spirit and can happen in anyone's life. This book shows what God's promises are, what to do to make them happen. The promises in the scriptures, from Abraham to what is revealed in the epistles, applies to believers today. The new covenant is not lacking in any blessing of the Old Testament. New Testament believers enjoy a better and improved covenant. Through the pages of this book, the reader will learn about the powerful Law of Seedtime and Harvest, the harmful effects of covetousness, how to reason together with God in prayer, how to recognize open doors, and how to appropriately deal with enemies of progress. This book can revolutionise your life, empower you to enjoy more victories, and move you into the place of your destiny.

Printed in Great Britain
by Amazon